I0408705

Trumping Frumpf

Buddy Winston

Copyright©2017Buddy Winston

All Rights Reserved

ISBN-13: 978-1546381051

ISBN-10: 1546381058

To the animals of the world left behind when humans are treated as less.

Special Book Thanks

John Horowitz, Kara Oh

Special Thanks

Ethel Psaty, Myron Mark Psaty, The Vilcabamba Organic Farmers, The Juice Factory, Astro, Cassie, Facebook Friends, Monte Schulz

PREFACE

When Donald Trump was leading the polls for the Republican presidential nomination at the end of 2015, the Huffington Post declared that they were moving their coverage of him from the *Politics* section to *Entertainment* because they considered his campaign to be merely a sideshow. Many of us felt the same and watched in horror as the stories never ceased and his popularity soared. The creative community was not only shocked by his rise to power but also frustrated that his ongoing antics became a major distraction as we were compelled to keep a watchful eye on the continual circus of events he instigated.

During this dark period in American history, I was writing my second novel but had trouble focusing, as my mind was busy following what I considered the degradation of democracy. Like most writers, I already possess a trunk full of my personal distractions that I have learned how to attenuate, but Trump's tyrannizing behavior was impossible for me to ignore. My artistic survival instinct kicked in and made me aware that my best hope of composing anything was to base it on the actual news items and anecdotes regarding Donald Trump that were diverting my attention.

Trumping Frumpf is not a book about Donald Trump. It is a story about dethroning an American dictator, utilizing many of the news articles critical of Trump as backdrop and character detail. Even though certain events in this book are straight out of the news media, Trumping Frumpf is a work of complete fiction. More so, Trumping Frumpf is a love story that will hopefully inspire the notion that the power of compassion will always defeat the dominance of depravity. The method of dethronement employed in this narrative is not only unconventional, but it is also a metaphor at best, the mechanism of which is ideally suited for our current commander in chief.

I hope you find *Trumping Frumpf* not only an entertaining take on the current state of society but also an inspiration to use love to help bring sanity back home.

*1

To the naked eye Thelma Timinsky was no rebel, but behind closed doors the forty-nine-year-old, fairly fetching housewife, maintained an illicit home business selling cannabis-infused gefilte fish to her neighborhood in Queens, New York. Thanks to Thelma's culinary creation many a Passover ceremony flowed as the participant's magnified hunger caused an accelerated reading of the traditional Haggadic passages to get right to the meal. Fifteen years ago Thelma and her older, congenial husband Norman, negotiated a fantastic deal on their current home because of a chronic leak in the basement the former owners couldn't figure out how to rectify. It turned out the basement shared a thick wall with a large, damp, antiquated catacomb replete with a pile of ancient skulls and rusted religious artifacts. It was Thelma's idea to cut open an arch in the wall to incorporate the extra space into what they used as a subterranean den. Instead of removing the skulls, Norman adorned them all with yarmulkes, which gave the room a quirky, synagogue atmosphere.

It was there in this eccentric den of antiquity Thelma was to hold her very first political rally. She felt she had her finger on the pulse of prevalent liberal concerns due to her ongoing subscription to the New Yorker magazine of which Norman coveted the cartoons. It all started when she met me, Sheldon Gross, claiming to have a secret power that inspired Thelma to dedicate herself to *the resistance*. She was opposing the flagrantly fraudulent election of the ultra-controversial president Richard J. Frumpf.

When Frumpf initially threw his *fat* into the ring, he was treated as comic relief by all of the media outlets that enjoyed the ratings boost. Then as one conventional candidate after another dropped out of the race due to their predictable partisan faux pas, Frumpf arrogantly declared he could butt-fuck an armadillo on Main Street and not lose voters. His statement was crude and unorthodox, but alarmingly accurate. The Middle American masses of the financially failing, educationally challenged, and pharmaceutically inclined embraced his raucous nonconformity, and along with some dubious Russian election tampering voted him in.

During his first few weeks in office the *complainer-in-chief* had already recklessly trivialized the constitution and was at war with his judicial branch of government who continually ruled against the executive orders he would inflict on the country; based on the fact the edicts infringed on American rights, and defied all logic. Heir Frumpf, as many citizens referred to him to point out his platform paralleled that of Hitler, was used to running his family business where he had the final word, and that word was usually "sue." To circumvent the media as well as even his own press secretary, Frumpf took to "tweeting" his knee-jerk opinions online at all hours of the evening; worrying the nation because most of his posts were petty, irrational, spiteful, and self-serving. He was preoccupied with denying any fact or figure that made him seem less respected than his predecessors. According to Frumpf, anyone who demeaned him was considered a total loser. He even labeled the greatest actress to ever live as overrated.

I met Thelma in the dairy section of the local Wal-Mart. I am moderately handsome, easily approachable, and presently perplexed whether to buy individually wrapped American cheese or a block of single sliced. When Thelma detected my state of confusion, she interjected by explaining that American cheese was not cheese at all, but carefully molded sludge that was a byproduct of making boot soles for the military discovered to possess a moldy, cheddar-esque flavor. She handed me a package of imported *Yarlsberg* insisting that due to the Volvo, Norwegian products have a reputation of being safer, which psychologically makes Yarlsberg taste purer. I inspected the package, and pointed out it was from Sweden, to which she claimed was directly next to Norway just as the American cheese was next to the Yarlsberg. Her quirky, semi-logical, rapid retort made me laugh, and so began our chat about all kinds of things as we moseyed towards the checkout.

That evening when Norman Timinsky arrived home from his job as a graphic artist for a company that is launching the *Flimsy Fork*; an eating utensil requiring the user to make numerous attempts to get the food to their mouth, thus being touted as the *greatest weight loss tool ever invented*, he found me sharing coffee and mandel bread with Thelma in his living room. Norman was a soft-spoken guy, comfortable within the marital paradigm of his wife sprinkling glitter on a life that was otherwise mundane. He greeted me with consternation, as he perceived Thelma was acting a different sort of odd than he was used to. He could never have guessed why.

Thelma blurted out that she had met me at the market, and I have the amazing ability to make someone's penis disappear. I would have recommended a more subtle approach, but I enjoyed how the shocking admission made Norman's bushy eyebrows raise. Thelma continued, confiding that the target of my incredible vanishing penis act required them to possess ample evil in their heart. She explained that I couldn't cause a man's cock to disappear just because I didn't like him or if he was dating a woman I fancied. I am embarrassed to say I attempted that once without success. It wasn't jealousy; I was trying to protect an ex-girlfriend from a serial dater. It was a good lesson in not being God.

Norman didn't know what to make of Thelma's sudden dick decimation declaration, and his first reaction was nervous laughter similar to someone who had just learned they were the prey of a practical joke. He was used to Thelma's crazy narratives; like the time she claimed that breathing the hair spray used at the beauty parlor was causing women to crave sushi.

Thelma explained the only way I could demonstrate my power was on a truly villainous target and said she understood if Norman was skeptical, as she was not completely convinced herself. Besides the issue that no man wants another guy to have vanishing power over his dick, Norman was a bit uneasy about the fact that Thelma brought home a stranger from the supermarket that made such peculiar claims. He also couldn't comprehend why anyone would deem such a power useful. Thelma then added the bombshell clarification; she had convinced me to help dethrone President Frumpf by what she playfully termed becoming his "thief-of-staff."

It didn't take a lot to sway me. Is there a greater pipe dream than to believe you can overpower rampant government corruption, and restore citizen's rights in the spirit of true democracy? It was this fantasy that inspired Thelma to suggest a trial run. All we needed was someone evil to test my power on to convince the couple I was the answer to eradicating a man who they considered to be the reincarnation of Adolph Hitler, a concept that would torment any Jew to take action. Accommodating Thelma's enthusiasm, Norman suggested Randolph Pewter, the director of marketing at Flimsy Fork. Apparently "Handy Randy," as he was known at the water cooler, earned the moniker due to his overly caressing back pats he gave the female employees. Randolph was a ball-buster, notorious for giving people nicknames based on whom he thought they resembled. Vic Johnson, the bearded accountant he often referred to as "Manson," asked him to refrain from calling him that, which only inspired Randolph to do it more often.

After engulfing stuffed cabbage and unduly sweet wine with the Timinskys I spent the night in the guestroom; a garret stuck in time as little Brucie Timinsky's room, Thelma and Norman's only child. Brucie ran away from home at the age of thirteen and flew off to Tibet. On the wall above his bed was a matador plaque featuring bullhorns the Timinsky's brought him back from their honeymoon in Spain, a vacation that took place five years after their marriage due to choosing to put every available dollar into the purchase of their current home. On the wall across the room was an old Bill Cosby '*I Spy*' poster of which Thelma had crossed out the word *Spy* and replaced it with RAPE.

It's been almost ten years since Brucie disappeared, and they've only heard from him once in a letter explaining that the neighborhood peer pressure to practice Judaism and get bar mitzvahed was destabilizing, but opened up his heart to seek balance through an alternative spiritual quest. He thanked them for the bar mitzvah cash that enabled him to buy a one-way ticket to Lhasa. Brucie already had a passport because Norman was planning on taking him to Israel to visit his sister, who moved there when she married an Israeli children's book author. They frantically attempted to track Brucie down, even sending Thelma's macho brother Jack to Tibet to retrieve him, but the closest they got was recovering a photo from a wall-collage of customer pics in a Nepalese eatery. At least Jack managed to quell every Jewish mother's primary concern; Brucie was eating. Jack fell in love, married a young, Chinese interpreter, and established a business importing Buddhist prayer flags and other Tibetan trinkets into the US.

The next morning it took three cups of coffee before I made up for the lack of sleep I experienced from being 6'4" on the abridged mattress of an adolescent. The bed also had one of those bloated foam pillows that could break a fall from a skyscraper. My neck is a fan of flat. On the way to his office in his gas-guzzling, blue Eldorado Cadillac, a hand-me-down from his attorney brother Murray, Norman and I devised a plan to deliver a package, at which time I could target Randolph's penis, and then leave before Handy Randy knew what hit him. I would drive home in the Eldorado, leaving Norman to catch a ride home with Vic "Manson" Johnson, who after learning about Randolph's malady would be ecstatic to drive anyone anywhere. Since coming in together would be a bit obvious, I killed some time at the *Deluxe Diner* across the street from Flimsy Fork headquarters. The location of Norman's drafting table offered him a bird's eye view of Randolph's desk. He was intrigued about our impending mission, even though he questioned his sanity for not only believing I could make a penis disappear, but for his willingness to participate in the outlandish endeavor.

I sat in a booth at the diner adjacent to a couple that was embroiled in a heated dispute. The wife expressed her dissatisfaction that the husband was not working, and the husband responded that any woman should be honored to support him due to his ability to please in bed. When the wife retorted that the only big dick in the marriage sits on top of his neck, the husband slapped her in the face. I was extremely perturbed by his act of violence as was the waitress standing nearby. I put down my cup of coffee and stared deep into the man's eyes. He snapped at me, asking what I was looking at, and referred to me as "queer face." I ignored the aspersion, placed some money on the table, and exited the diner. While walking across the street, I could hear the man screaming in shock, obviously reacting to the realization he no longer had a dick.

When I informed Norman what had transpired, I also explained that my power needed to regenerate before I could vanish another. It was one dick a day. He was amused by the tale, relieved he was off the hook, but completely lost faith in the reality of my ability. He did wonder why I would put so much energy into such a freakish sham.

When Norman arrived home that night, Thelma admitted that she too was skeptical of my self-proclaimed talent, blaming her gullibility on her over-enthusiastic desire to rid the world of Frumpf. All the penis talk had a stimulating effect on the couple, rousing them to engage in their first sexual encounter in weeks.

Everyone loves a sunny Saturday morning. Before Thelma was out of bed, Norman had already returned from the bagel store with a freshly baked variety, including some Nova Scotia salmon and cream cheese. He stepped around the room with a whimsical, Astaire-like prance, while he brewed the coffee, and placed the breakfast goodies on the appropriate platters. Although their previous night's tepid sexual liaison lasted the usual couple of minutes, due in part to the reality they were both orgasmically expeditious, the physical connection made him feel they were back on track. So much so that when Thelma entered the kitchen in her robe, Norman picked up a bagel, and suggestively poked his finger in and out of the hole. Thelma laughed and imparted she hoped her vagina didn't remind him of a bagel, to which he replied he hoped his small finger didn't remind her of his cock.

During breakfast, Thelma told Norman she had a dream about me and wondered if they should have given me the benefit of the doubt and another chance to prove my abilities. Norman asked if he should be concerned after last night's encounter that she dreamed about someone that could make a dick disappear. Thelma scooped her finger in the tub of cream cheese, then slowly licked it off with her elongated tongue, and replied,

"As I always tell you Norman, worrying doesn't help anything."

Norman's Cadillac pulled up in front of a seedy apartment building where a teenager wearing a Spiderman t-shirt was hawking porn DVDs. The sign on the table read: PORN IN THE MORN. Inside the car, Norman asked Thelma if she was sure they were in the right place. She claimed I supposedly inherited the apartment from my late mother and emphasized it was an exclusive building in its heyday. Norman wondered aloud if heyday was *hey* or *hay*. Thelma said it was spelled *hey,* and couldn't imagine former prosperous times denoted by the image of straw. As they passed by the DVD stand, Norman noticeably perused some of the racy covers.

The building elevator has been out of service for two years because the last time a repairman attempted to inspect it, he was robbed. When they got to the 8th floor, Norman was out of breath. Thelma was fine because three days a week she does 'Bloga,' a form of exercise where participants engage in whatever athletic activity the blog suggests for that day. Thelma confirmed the apartment number on a piece of paper she retrieved from her purse and knocked on the door. The doors to the other two apartments opened simultaneously exposing seedy looking inhabitants who began to size up the couple. Uncomfortable, Norman attempted to feign a Jehovah Witness affiliation by asking them if they wanted to have eternal-life. To their relief, the door to my apartment finally opened, and I guided them both inside.

The faded wallpaper of the interior depicted blooming lilacs, images that helped distract from the fact my abode is devoid of furniture except for a stained, antique, plush purple velvet couch, and a wide array of crystals that sit haphazardly all over the room's floor and windowsills. I motioned for the couple to sit on the sofa and then walked into the dimly lit kitchen to retrieve chipped mugs of coffee and a small plate of Ritz crackers that were topped with chunks of Yarlsberg cheese. I explained that the crystals had belonged to my self-proclaimed Shaman priestess mother. Then I told a story about the time a guy attempted to rape her while she was in an Ayahuasca-induced trance trying to help heal his anger issues. I was a teenager at the time, and when I came home and witnessed the assault, I panicked and hit the guy over the head with the first thing I saw, a *Labradorite crystal wand*. I alleged that when the wand came in contact with the assailant's head the whole room vibrated and burst into what I called visual prismatic chaos. A few seconds later after the spectacle ceased, the guy was somehow devoid of his penis. He violently demanded I use the wand to make it come back, but I couldn't because I had no clue how to do that. Having felt the odd turbulence, the neighbors entered the apartment in what was an altered state and escorted the man away. Norman stared into my eyes as if I told him the Tooth Fairy was a winged dominatrix and Big Foot was her best customer.

"Your Shaman Priestess mom went into a trance to stop a guys anger, but as he tried to rape her you hit him with a magic wand and made his penis disappear," asked Norman.

"I don't know if the wand was magic, because ever since then I have had this power," I replied.

Norman's mind raced with a million unanswered questions about the neighbors, the fate of the guy, etc. Thelma simply asked if I had any cream for her coffee.

Back home, Thelma and Norman reclined in bed watching Schindler's list on the flat screen. Thelma said if there is any way to stop a despot like Frumpf they had to try. Norman acquiesced but insisted if I fail to make Randolph's dick disappear during tomorrow morning's office meeting he is done with this whole penis nonsense, and finished with me.

The new plan was to have me barge into the *Flimsy Fork* morning staff meeting acting lost. Norman would make sure to sit to the right of Randolph so I would know whom to target. I revealed that the duration of time a penis would vanish varied depending on how evil the target is and how appalled I am about the miscreant's behavior. I predicted that in the case of Randolph it would last only a day or so.

As the morning meeting progressed, Norman kept checking his watch, again doubting I would show up and prove myself. Arnold Tipman, a short, southern attorney for the company, addressed the group regarding a copyright issue affecting the product. Randolph shushed everyone and asked them to let "Jeff Sessions" speak. Some laughed out of embarrassment, but Arnold was not pleased about being compared to the corrupt, attorney general. Suddenly the door to the room opened revealing me. I exchanged a quick glance with Norman and followed his eyes to the left where Randolph sat. I looked deep into Randolph's eyes, and then excused myself claiming I was in the wrong office. Roughly a minute later Randolph noticed something about his groin felt very peculiar. He stood up in dismay, quickly exited the room, and rushed to the bathroom to check his groin. His scream was heard throughout the building. Norman was astounded to learn my power was authentic.

In post-coital embrace Norman voiced his concern that the tale of a guy losing his dick turned Thelma on. Thelma was ecstatic that my power was on the level. She couldn't wait to take the next step in our plan to save the country from Frumpf, and went even further claiming we were about to save the whole fucking world.

Australia, Mexico, and Iran were already up in arms over Frumpf's narcissistic, immature actions. He signed executive orders that canceled environmental protection laws, and he now appointed the former head of a major oil company as his secretary of state. Most of that happened within his first two weeks in office.

As cars pulled up and parked in front of the Timinsky home, it was obvious something out of the ordinary was taking place. A group of people carrying potluck items marched into the house. Thelma had not told the folks now gathering in her basement den why exactly she called this meeting to order except she had an amazing plan to stop Frumpf. The night before, the president passed a law banning Muslims from America without going through the proper vetting or legal channels. This careless act of blatant prejudice created complete chaos at the airports, which inspired masses of protestors to show up to offer support to the oppressed individuals. Citizens all over the country were scrounging for any measure that could help remove Frumpf from office, so the neighborhood turnout was large.

Almost twenty-five people packed into the den, most of them fans of Thelma's marijuana gefilte fish, to hear the strategy she had in mind. Thelma served her famous dish, reasoning that people would be more receptive to what she was about to announce if they were stoned. After an hour of kibitzing, noshing, and drinking, Thelma rang a Tibetan bell her brother Jack once brought her back from his travels. Everyone began to quiet down and gave her their undivided attention.

Thelma commenced her speech,

"As many of you are aware our newly appointed President Richard Frumpf is not only an ignoramus but an evil dictator that hopes to take America down a path of extreme racism and environmental demise. You don't have to be Jewish to understand the potential disaster that can occur if we allow a fascist power to continue to rise."

Everyone clapped and hailed out blurbs of support.

She continued, "What I am about to share will not only seem preposterous but given the altered state most of you are in right now might cause you to laugh dismissively."

Some people laughed in anticipation of her secret.

She went on, "Please welcome my friend, and soon to be the savior of our planet, Ryan Clark."

Thelma and I previously agreed not to use my real name for obvious reasons. I stepped to the front of the crowd, and after a moment of shy hesitation began to state my piece,

"Thank you all for coming. I imagine we are all gathered here for the same reason; to resist Richard J. Frumpf."

Everyone applauded and cheered their endorsement.

"I think I have a way to help. A bit unconventional maybe, but given the right circumstances it should prove to be more than effective."

I again hesitated, knowing they would be somewhat shocked. I continued,

"So here it is; I have a way I can make Frumpf's penis disappear."

The audience laughed as if I was making a joke.

"I told you it was unconventional," I said.

They laughed again.

Thelma interjected, "He's not joking. He can really do this."

The crowd turned silent and stared in our direction as if we announced we would be serving Ebola ice cream. A tall man, Steve Tanenbaum, broke the silence,

"This is what you called us here for? Seriously, your answer to ousting Frumpf is an overzealous mohel?"

The crowd laughed at the circumcision reference. Thelma interrupted,

"I realize how outlandish this sounds, but he has proven he can do this. He can actually make an evil man's penis vanish just by looking at him."

Tanenbaum immediately crossed his legs and covered his crotch with his hands, which put the crowd in hysterics.

When the laughter died down Thelma continued,

"Maybe the funny fish was a bad idea because I think you are all too stoned to believe in this."

Lenny Koslow chimed in,

"Your guy is a regular David *Cock*erfield."

The crowd wouldn't let up with the ridicule and was laughing so hard the pile of skulls in the corner toppled causing everyone to go,

"Oooohhh."

Noshing on leftover potluck an hour later, Thelma, Norman, Faye Siegel (a short, spunky seamstress) and I, sat in the kitchen discussing the evening. Faye revealed how sorry she was the meeting didn't go well but was curious why we even needed the crowd if I can do what I say. Thelma pointed out getting to the President was no easy task, especially the close proximity I needed to stare right into his beady eyes. She said she was also hoping for some positive feedback to get us motivated. Faye asked me how many penises I had made disappear. My answer was four. The guy who tried to rape my mom, the jerk at the diner the other day, Handy Randy, and one I said I didn't want to talk about for personal reasons.

"More personal than making people's penis vanish," Thelma asked.

She wanted to know that if there were only four, how come I knew so much about the process; like how much evil the target needed to have, and how long it would last? I told her the sensibilities regarding what to expect came with the power, adding it may have been some divine gift or a bad curse. Being brought up by a mother who was open to psychotropic plants and energy crystals made me amenable to all theories. I was quite uncomfortable with the power and never planned to use it again until Thelma zealously presented me with the prospect of ridding the world of Frumpf.

Peter Snopes was a retired FBI agent, living in the suburbs of Hoboken, New Jersey, the birthplace of Frank Sinatra. Beneath his tumefied frame was the muscular physique he formerly used to stand his ground against subversives. Snopes survived on his government pension and spent most of his free time attempting to propagate a designer vegetable through the grafting of conventional plants. His dream was not of riches but a desire for his legacy to be that of an inventor of something wholesome, instead of an agent of what he considered to be a false democracy. Snopes had ongoing conflicting issues about his former job because he was well aware that his organization too often skirted the law, or mutated moral decency to conduct their missions. The self-empowerment the bureau possessed based on potential domestic terror prevention was in his eyes an attack on civil liberties, religious freedom, and numerous other constitutional rights.

Snopes had a daughter Ella who ran a modeling agency for plus-sized gals. They exchanged holiday greetings through email, but since he was gone most of her childhood they didn't share a very close bond; something Snopes sincerely regretted. Ella never cashed the overly generous Christmas and birthday checks he sent her. Her mother Inga died of a sudden heart attack at the age of thirty-five causing fifteen-year-old Ella to be raised by her grandmother. Somewhere in the back of her mind, Ella wondered if the real story about her mom's death didn't have something to do with Snopes' FBI involvement.

Outside of his horticulture Snopes was not very domestic. While out purchasing the usual ready-cooked barbeque chicken at the local market a tabloid news cover caught his attention. It was a blurry photo of a man at a diner booth with a caption that read,

DOMESTIC DISPUTE IN DINER ENDS IN HUSBAND'S VANISHING PENIS.

Snopes shook his head in disbelief, acknowledging to himself the absurdity of the tabloids, and drove off in his truck.

*3

The water cooler at Flimsy Fork was buzzing. Everyone was huddled together whispering their take on what happened to Handy Randy.

"I think the pressure of the job was too much for him; he was such a dick I'm surprised he didn't disappear completely."

"I have to admit that if anyone deserved it, it was him."

"What a weird delusion, how do we act normal when he comes back in?"

"I hear they're going to let him go, and as a women, I'm offended that as soon as you don't have a dick, you lose your job."

Everyone laughed.

I'm not joking," she added.

To ward off attention to himself Norman remained silent. He had already taken a bold chance by visiting Randolph at the hospital. According to the doctor, who thought he was talking to Randolph's brother, his dick was gone for a day and is now back. Experts were brought in who wanted to run experiments on Randolph's crotch to understand the odd phenomenon. Although Randolph wanted to know what happened as well, and how to prevent it from reoccurring, he refused to allow further probing. When Randolph returned to the office that day he was a changed man. He no longer dared to ridicule anyone with nicknames or appear arrogant, in fear the retaliation of dick jokes was too much to bear. Even without a word uttered his coworker's attempt not to mention the elephant in the room created an obvious, uncomfortable vibe. My little stunt had powerful repercussions, and Norman was not used to being part of such an active camarilla.

Maryanne Covert was a rabid pit-bull in the form of a once marginally attractive woman. The bags under her eyes were big enough to carry around a litany of excuses, responses, and absurd rhetoric that angered the most experienced newscasters, and caused the nation a great deal of concern because she was Frumpf's principal spokesperson. In defense of another one of the president's long list of lies, today she claimed he was voicing "alternative facts." Whether it was due to the way she swallowed the term as if it had just cum in her mouth, or that the news anchor was facing the reality that the presidency was now a parody of itself, he broke out in uncontrollable hysterics, causing the network to pause the interview while he pulled himself together. Covert was now a celebrity, and her main talent was abstracting every stupid thing Frumpf said on a regular basis, and sanitizing it. Her methods were outrageous, yet predictable. When she was at a loss for words, she would site rumored misconduct of past presidents. Covert's routine Frumpf defense was insisting that the public misunderstood his intent.

Recently, while Frumpf was about to step up to the podium in the Rose Garden to give a speech about the Holocaust, the hot microphone caught him joking,

"I may not be sure about the Holocaust, but I certainly knew what a ho cost."

When this statement went viral on the Internet, it caused major outrage all over the world. Covert's best attempt at softening the blow had her claiming Frumpf actually said, "home cost," and that the rest of the statement said Frumpf hoped all Jewish people felt at home in America. It didn't help that the during that same week Frumpf's press secretary made the outrageous claim that Hitler never gassed his citizens.

Quite a few people that attended Thelma's home rally were now intrigued with our presentation when through the grapevine they heard tales of recent events where a man's penis was said to have disappeared. They contacted her with an apology and asked what they could do to help. It wasn't just that rumors validated my claim, it was also Frumpf was becoming more dangerous. He had threatened a nuclear war with N. Korea, and at this point, people would welcome a holographic knight on a silver unicorn if it represented even the slightest hope the American dictator could be stopped.

Raring to rescue the planet, Thelma went to the beauty parlor to have her highlights done. While in the coiffing chair she fantasized she was now part of a famous rebellion and wanted to look her best when we wound up on the cover of Time Magazine. The date had been set, and in two days Thelma, Faye, Edna Finkelbrook (a neighbor who owned a cut-rate travel agency), and I, were heading to Philadelphia where Frumpf was scheduled to give a speech to the teacher's union about why his inexperienced billionaire nominee to head the department of education would revolutionize learning, and turn America into the smartest country in the world again. The plan was for me to pose a question, and while exchanging glances with Frumpf turn him into what Thelma now calls the *Dicklesstator*.

That night Thelma prepared a candlelight dinner, put on her finest dress and nibbled on some spiked gefilte fish while waiting for Norman to come home from work. When Norman entered the house he was tantalized by the uncommon romantic atmosphere Thelma had created. Although she loves Norman, their relationship was temperate and uneventful. She decided to attempt to awaken a spark. Norman's eyes announced he was pleased, but Thelma sensed something was wrong and quizzed him about it. As they sipped wine, Norman explained there was an investigator at Flimsy Fork that afternoon interviewing workers about Handy Randy's vanishing penis episode. Since no one knew the real story except for him, he felt like the investigator may have picked up on Norman's guilt. Norman, of course, didn't admit to anything, and may have been imagining things, but it made him feel uneasy so he suggested maybe they should put off the whole plan until the heat died down. He was also concerned that some of the people from her rally might spill the beans and lead the authorities to them.

"Too much funny fish to deal with any distress Norman," she said to the tune of a song he didn't recognize.

Norman immediately changed the subject to how beautiful Thelma looked. They continued to dine, wine, and unwind until the candles were mere puddles. Thelma claimed she knew how to make Norman forget everything and got on her knees in front of him. Whether it was a long day at work, worries about the Frumpf scheme or too much wine, Norman fell asleep mid-blow.

As it turned out, Norman's concerns might have ended on their own, as I was nowhere to be found for the following week. Thelma and Norman stopped by my apartment a couple of times leaving notes under the door, but not a word back from me. At first, they presumed I was just reneging on my participation in taking down Frumpf, but then they speculated that maybe someone turned me in. The truth was impossible for them to establish, so they just let it go, and went on with their normal life.

As Thelma followed the degradation of democracy in the news, she longed to have my power back in her midst. Frumpf was way out of control. At a Christian prayer breakfast, he promised to end the separation of church and state. The conservative right, who held the majority of seats in both the house and senate, were coercing him to carry out their most heavy-handed corporate agenda. It was the perfect political ploy figuring once Frumpf was impeached or assassinated they could blame all the new laws on him, and maintain continuous rule based on the voter restrictions and gerrymandering stacked in their favor. The Democrats were seen as spineless, obsolete representatives, and unless something could be done immediately to change the dynamics America would succumb to totalitarian rule. Many secret online trolls had been organized to spread false information to thwart the liberal resistance. Thelma got lost in a sea of continuous political blogs. She needed more out of life and wanted to change history. She was sure I was the ticket, and she needed to find me to get me back on board.

It had been a momentous morning for Snopes as one of his experimental plants appeared to be producing something new. It was a combination of kale and cucumber, what he would refer to as Cuka. His mind drifted off thinking about Cuka juice, a coveted beverage that would cure Cancer and even Alzheimer's. He visualized a poster of a gorgeous woman, leaning against an old barn, drinking the green translucent beverage in an extremely satisfied way. He came back to earth realizing that the plant was small, and the chances that the Cuka would grow large enough even to pass as saliva were minimal. Nevertheless, it was a call for a celebration, so he went to the local market to pick up a couple of bottles of Modelo Light, a beer he learned to love after being given one by a Mexican horticulturist who helped him set up his garden. Snopes was originally a Heineken man after visiting the brewery in Holland. The freshly brewed version was potent and delicious, much more so than the inferior backwash that was sold in the states. Even so, the taste was familiar enough to remind him of not only the beer, but his late wife Irma who rarely drank, but went overboard that day at the brewery performing a well-received, impromptu song and dance routine for everyone there. He will occasionally suffer through drinking one just to reminisce.

Instead of grabbing the usual two bottles from the beer fridge, Snopes opted for the whole sixer because they now plastic shrink-wrap it. It was never an issue of money, but if he bought six, he would drink six. His willpower diminished with each bottle and if he drank all of them he would wind up making prank calls to former agent pals to scare the hell out of them. He once called Wallace Patterson using a heavy middle-eastern accent and claimed Wallace was the agent who caused the death of his family. When Wallace responded with trepidation, he would break out in laughter, and call "Wally" a wuss. But today was no normal day because it marked the birth of Cuka, and Snopes felt carelessly festive. At the checkout counter, he glanced at the nearby tabloid and noticed another story about a man and a vanishing penis. He bought the paper as well.

Years ago. I followed my mother's wishes and spread her ashes all around the overly organized cemetery she'd chosen. At the time it felt callous, but now I get it. No matter which gravestone I honor, her spirit mingles with it.

"Feed my deceased body to the dogs," she used to say, "so that one less precious animal goes hungry in the night."

Although I shared her concern for the animals of the world, that I couldn't do. Katie Gross was only five when my grandparents emigrated from Romania, yet her recollection of her gypsy roots was that of a historian. It was impossible to tell if her proclamations regarding the soul derived from ancient wisdom or her own bold prescience. Not that it mattered because as she used to say,

"Wisdom is wisdom if the wisdom works."

My mom had a wild sense of humor and insisted that my dad died at childbirth. She assured me that his disappearance when I was born was a blessing, and welcomed me to trace him down, but I never did. Today I was here to trace her down. She used to say that when I speak to her, I speak to my own heart, and my heart needed talking to right now.

"What should I do mother? He is not only a thoughtless, dangerous man; he could cause the end of the world. If I go through with this and use my power, he's evil enough to never get his penis back. A man whose whole identity is caught up in his sexuality could die from this. I would possibly be assassinating the President of the United States."

A strong wind blew through the necropolis lifting one white rose from a nearby grave right into my hand. As I clenched my fingers around it, I was cut by a thorn. My mother also used to say,

"To hold onto beauty, one must be willing to endure the pain."

*8

At the supermarket, I spotted Thelma inspecting different bottles of French dressing. I stepped up from behind, and commented,

"You know, there's nothing French about that stuff."

Thelma turned around and responded in delight,

"Is that so?"

"Oh yeah, it's about as French as deep fried string potatoes, or cleaning the inside of someone's mouth with your tongue when you kiss," I said.

"Wow, where do you get a job like that," she joked.

"If it were me, I'd opt for Russian dressing, which is just ketchup and mayo."

Thelma thanked me for the tip but said due to Russia's apparent manipulation of the Frumpf election she is sticking with France right now. She then asked where I had been. I suggested we go for a cup of coffee because we have a lot to 'Ketchup' on. Thelma acted like that was the funniest thing she'd ever heard, but her glee was actually a product of our reunion.

Now on his fifth Modelo, Snopes' willpower was history. The previous four bottles were lined up on the table in front of him. The news on the flat screen reported a failed military raid in Yemen in which an eight-year-old girl and a Navy Seal were killed. A Democratic senator blamed the incidence on Frumpf's unwillingness to attend strategic military briefings and rushing to action before all intel was complete. Snopes was so upset he knocked the four bottles over like dominos. Then when Covert, Frumpf's bride of Frankenstein spokeswoman, claimed the people were killed because recent public protests have put the president off of his game, Snopes lost it.

"Off his fucking game?! The presidency is not a fucking game; this ain't scrabble lady. Oh excuse me world, but I just nuked Tehran because my opponent got gin rummy. Had you not distracted me my polluting pipeline wouldn't have been shoved up the Native American's ass," he yelled.

The sound of the doorbell interrupted his pickled rant. Snopes picked up the remote to mute the sound, and after a few failed attempts he finally hit the right button. When he opened the door, his whole world came to a halt. His eyes weren't teary but were glazed with the precipitation of sincere emotion. He ran his hand through his grayish white hair like a comb and presented the kind of smile that was as much forced, as it was undeniable. Standing before him was his daughter.

"Ella, this is so unexpected," he muttered.

"Is this a bad time," she inquired.

Then after perceptively sizing up his condition, asked,

"Are you drunk on a Tuesday afternoon?"

Snopes opened his arms inviting a hug, and Ella cautiously entered the embrace. There was no denying Ella was large, not plump, fat, or flabby, but six feet tall, and large framed like her dad. Her hazel eyes emanated wisdom, and her white toothy smile could blind the devil. At this very moment, as she sat in the kitchen with her intoxicated father she hadn't seen in years, her smile was hidden beneath an expression of concern.

"So you're telling me you're drunk because you made a biological breakthrough with a cucumber?" She asked.

"The way you say it doesn't sound auspicious at all. In a nutshell, though yes, but the goal was not to be this intoxicated," he claimed.

"So, Dad, you're saying you were overwhelmed by the discovery?"

"Not exactly Ella. You see, I rarely drink alcohol, and when I do, I buy only two beers at a time to ensure I don't allow my weakened resistance to take it further. The makers of my favorite beer now shrink-wrap the six-pack, so it is much more difficult to purchase only a couple. I fell for their commercial scheme, and the next thing you know..."

"Not very ecological. Do you realize how much plastic has entered the environment? We're killing all the wildlife and poisoning ourselves, so someone like you will buy more beer? That's crazy, don't you think?" She lectured.

"Everything is out of balance in the world right now, Ella. The leader of our country can't spell and thinks the Federal Reserve is a type of wine. He's creating total havoc, and completely disregarding the constitution. And! There's no one with power willing to stop him. The United States of America has been taken over by a tyrant with the brain of a corpse. Remember a few weeks ago when the biggest concern in the country was where a tranny could go to the bathroom? Not anymore," he said.

Ella took in his tirade and replied,

"The correct term is transgender, dad, and I do understand. My agency deals in plus size models and Frumpf appears capable of making large women illegal."

*10

As she bit into a thick grilled cheese at the Deluxe Diner across the street from Flimsy Fork headquarters, Thelma's sandwich dripped all over her wrists while I watched with amusement.

"Was I right or not? Could a grilled cheese be any more decadent than that," I asked.

Thelma put the sandwich down on the plate and used a napkin to wipe the mess off of her arms.

"I'm not sure Swiss or cheddar wouldn't be tastier, and much less messy for that matter, but it is quite good. So Sheldon, are you going to tell me what's going on or not?"

I laid out all of my fears about our plot,

"What if the CIA has detectors that could trace whose eyes the vibrations come from? What if I get nervous and the bodyguards pick up on it? What if the loss of Frumpf's penis causes him to lash out at the world with a nuclear bomb?"

While Thelma digested the combination of my questions and the grilled cheese, I noticed the couple from the other day entering the diner. The husband no longer appeared to be dickless and seemed to be in harmony with his wife now. As they sat in a nearby booth, the husband and I exchanged glances. I was concerned he would recognize me as the *pocket rocket shocker,* but he merely smiled and went about his business. The realization I may have saved this couple's marriage with my temporary penis shenanigan caused me to straighten my posture, and blurt out a declaration,

"I'll do it, I will make the president's..."

I catch myself before I carelessly declare my power within ears reach of my last victim, and finished my sentence in a whisper,

"...penis disappear."

Thelma looked pleased that her de-Frumpfing hopes were back in action, and told me that I made the right choice.

"I hope so," I said as I looked at my previous target.

Ella exited the bathroom with Snopes' tabloid newspapers in her hand.

"What is with all these vanishing penis headlines, dad? Last I remember you read books," she lamented.

"The other day I was at that diner. The waitress swore it happened. She witnessed it, one of the disappearing penis episodes," Snopes claimed.

"Now you work for what, the missing penis bureau? I thought you were retired?" She asked.

"I'm bored," he admitted.

Ribbing him, she said, "Oh, I would have thought mutating vegetables was exciting."

Snopes chuckled. "There's a lot of waiting, and something about this penis caper has my investigative intuition on alert."

Ella reached into her purse and pulled out a fat envelope.

Snopes' eyes narrowed.

"They're all the checks you've been sending me. I don't need your money dad. You don't have to feel guilty about neglecting me. Whatever you did or didn't do when I was a child helped me become who I am, and I am happy with me," she insisted.

Snopes immediately changed the subject and asked her if she was in a relationship.

"Yes dad, and you would like her. She's smart, funny, and has an affinity for cucumbers," she said.

Snopes was speechless.

"I have to get back to work. Call me soon, and come meet Angela."

"You never said why you came here today." Snopes said.

"If there's one positive thing I've noticed about Frumpf's presidency, it makes people realize that we have to stick closer together. Let's do that."

She gave him a hug and headed for the door.

Protesters, mostly women, have flooded the streets of New York. Many are wearing mop hats to *remonstrate* a statement made to the press by a Republican senator that a woman's place in society was to "mop and glow."

Many of the participants carried posters:

LET'S CLEAN UP THE SENATE FLOOR

A WOMAN'S PLACE IS IN THE white **HOUSE**

Thelma and I looked like members of a cartoon rock band in our mop hats as we took part in the march. She loathed the inferior way women were treated and thought participating would give me the inspiration to go through with our plan to what we have now nicknamed *Operation Jerkumcision*. I suggested we no longer refer to Frumpf by his name, and instead use a variety of sobriquets; her favorite being *Shitler*.

As we began to march, I noticed a red rusty van pull up on the curb. A couple of rogues disembarked with what appeared to be cans of spray paint. They slapped on mop hats and rudely pushed through the crowd making a beeline for a large storefront window. For some reason, I was compelled to head in the same direction. Thelma tagged along unsure about where I was rushing. As we all reached the storefront, the two guys wielded their paint cans towards the window. I managed to exchange glances with one of them. As the other started to spray an obscene epitaph on the glass, his co-conspirator dropped his can on the ground and screamed at the top of his lungs.

The evening news used the epitaph as a sign the protestors were unruly and just as prejudice as the Senator they were protesting. As we drank lattes on a park bench, I told Thelma my intuition was working overtime when I spied the arrival of the guys in the van. I headed for the window on instinct alone and decided if I looked the guy in the eye with the intent of making his dick disappear it would only work if the guy were truly evil. Thelma understood but suggested it may be better to keep the power under wraps until we complete our mission with Frumpf. I claimed it was almost impossible not to act, and expressed concern that the more I used the power, the more I felt inclined to do so. It almost felt like it was beginning to control me.

Even the New York Post ran a story about the rash of penis disappearances. When Snopes saw the crotch bandit had struck again, he went online and researched everything he could on the subject. The first thing he came across was an article about *Penis Panic*. Apparently, in the sixteenth-century countries such as Britain and Germany experienced a flood of frenzied witch hunts that ended in the execution of suspects accused of being sorcerers that had the power to steal a man's cock. Said to stem from a hysteria based on deep-rooted psychological fears regarding loss of status, sexual ability, or patriarchal power, Penis Panic was an epidemic. The men believed female witches were fornicating with the devil giving them sinister abilities to control crops and crotches. Snopes' findings also included something called *Koro*, which still exists in Southern China and Southeast Asia where men believe their penis is shrinking, and will eventually retreat into their bodies, and disappear. Although practitioners of Chinese medicine attributed it to the waning of male energy and the ingesting of pork infected with swine flu, many men thought of it as a curse, and tied red strings around their dick to stop the disappearance, a practice that often caused them actual problems with their privates. In Africa, when a man imagined his cock began to shrink he would accuse a nearby person as if they were pointing out a pickpocket, or in this case a *dickpocke*t, causing crowds to apprehend, and often batter the innocent victim sometimes to death. Now convinced *Genital Retraction Syndrome* was at least something men of the world feared, Snopes decided to step up his investigation.

The office of the FBI in New York was nowhere near as pretentious as the building in Langley. Snopes made an appointment with his old friend and local bureau chief, Parker Lice. Lice was macho and sure of himself enough that he never bothered to change his last name. He was fond of Snopes and owed him gratitude based on an incident in which Snopes took the blame for a procedural error that might have hindered Lice's ensuing promotion. Snopes was retiring anyway, so he stepped in to protect his friend. The meeting was about temporary reinstatement, so that Snopes could utilize all of the bureau's intelligence resources to follow up on the penis caper. Lice was overly curious why Snopes was so interested in other men's penises, offering instead to fix him up with his wife's sister who was recently divorced, and "horny as hell." Snopes assured him his focus had nothing to do with the genitalia itself, and he had a strong hunch the story was about way more than cocks. He explained his horticulture hobby was like watching snails race, and if he didn't involve himself in something soon he would delve into *Second Life*, an online virtual community that sucks people in and replaces their need for real human interaction. Lice used his position to reinstate Snopes' clearance on a limited basis and jokingly referred to the new position as agent in charge of cocks and robbers. Everyone has a dick joke in them.

*14

Ayahuasca is a traditional spiritual medicine used for ceremonial purposes by the indigenous people of the Amazon. Early Christian missionaries saw the psychotropic drink as the handiwork of the devil, but thought the same thing about any spiritual custom that circumvented the Bible. The difference is, indigenous medicines were not designed for the religious goal of *compos mentis,* and instead of control allowed the mind to expand beyond the pew. My mother was an avid Ayahuasca practitioner, and occasionally shared with me the visions and philosophies she experienced on her sacred journeys. She claimed there were other dimensions of existence, and that Ayahuasca was a peek into that divine fabric. She encouraged me to question the emphatic theories promoted by conventional schools of thought, and claimed phenomena like déjà vu were more prophetically oriented than conventional judgment suggested. I joked that I felt like she told me that before.

With my mother's spirit in mind, I proposed to Thelma and Norman that before we set out to save the world, we should experience a sacrament that might inspire revelations we may have overlooked. Norman said he is afraid to hallucinate and that he is already having visions they all wind up in prison. Thelma saw it as a first step out of the mundane, declaring her spirituality could use a good kick in the ass. She suggested we journey in the den where we would not be bothered, proclaiming the catacombs would add a mystical atmosphere to the ritual.

Thelma and I sat on pillows we had placed on the floor. A lone glass cup-candle flickered against the wall in the corner of the room. We originally set it in the catacombs, but the light glimmering off of the skulls felt a bit too eerie. I encouraged Thelma to go easy on the dosage, but she insisted on drinking an equal amount to me. Her reasoning was she didn't want to miss out on any of what she referred to as the "cosmic hoobeedo." Thelma loved to make up fun terms for everything. As the medicine slowly took effect, we sat in complete silence.

*15

A cacophony of commotion was taking place on the fifth floor of Manhattan's Lennox Hill hospital where a hoard of physicians was gathered around the bed of Glen Riker. Riker is the spray paint demon whose penis I eradicated at the march. Turns out, unbeknownst to everyone, especially me, that Riker had once raped an underage girl and had gotten away with it, until now. Because of his level of evil, his penis may be gone forever, and needed medical treatment to deal with urination. He was emphatic the doctors figure out a way to make his genitals come back and was desperate to understand how this could happen to him, or anyone for that matter.

Snopes entered the ruckus, requesting to speak with the physician in charge. Dr. Andrew Weller had the perfect name for his profession. When Snopes presented his credentials, Weller took him to a private office to discuss recent events. Snopes learned that although there are many tales and superstitions throughout history regarding vanishing genitalia, Weller had never heard of an actual occurrence in modern times until now. Snopes was curious if the doctor was familiar with the other two recent cases. Weller had read those reports and found the whole thing to be outside his realm of science. He wondered if it might not be a reaction to environmental causes, and even the effects of Fukushima fallout. Snopes was fascinated by the possibility radiation leakage from the crippled Japanese nuclear power plant could have played a role, but maintained the scenario was too Godzilla-like. He argued that even if the science supported plutonium's ability to abracadabra someone's genitals, it still didn't explain how some got them back. The doctor admitted the supposition was farfetched, but at this time no theory was plausible. He then quipped they should at least be thankful it didn't appear to be contagious.

Thelma was lying on the floor with her eyes closed quietly humming the Blue Danube Waltz. I paced the room with a crystal held up against my forehead with my right hand. My mind could not let go of the recent penile events, and I was all over the map regarding my responsibility to humanity on the whole, and my culpability as a self-appointed punisher of evil. As imposing as my thoughts became, I was cognizant it was all part of the process.

Thelma on the other hand was now humming Beethoven's Fifth and broke the silence to question whether it was Beethoven himself who titled his songs as numerical movements.

"Not very creative titling for a guy who composed all that shit," she said.

She laughed at her own statement, saying she thought a spiritual journey would have been different. She imagined it more like a séance. To underline the absurdity of her comment, she said,

"What if we could actually contact Ludwig and ask him?"

Her sudden outburst caused her to laugh uncontrollably, and it was impossible not to laugh along. I'm not sure this is what the original Shamans had in mind. When the hysteria subsided, we both needed to catch our breath. Thelma wondered if the possibility that the future of humankind rested on our plan to make the president's dick disappear was too much to fathom. She then asked if I thought Gandhi might have laughed his way to liberation. As she went on questioning, I sat there thinking about my mother, the cemetery rose, and what she would say to shed light on my quandary.

Thelma then said,

"What if by movement Beethoven meant something else? Maybe he was giving us a clue that his music could transport us. Do you think Ludwig did Ayahuasca?"

As Thelma was on a cerebral journey, I was on a collision course with my heart. In its deepest sanctum, unconditional love was the conceptual Holy Grail, but who could maintain an unmitigated regard for a dishonest despot? Would preventing a megalomaniac from crippling the planet be considered an act of love towards even him? In his unexpected dicklessness would he see the light to a more compassionate future? Is maiming for the greater good the rationalization all warriors use to justify their actions? By castrating the president am I just another warmongering general drunk on the delusion of saving humanity? No wonder unconditional love is so scarce, it is almost impossible to unravel.

Thelma looked at me as if she could hear my thoughts and said,

"Sheldon, to every trend there is an anti-trend. There is no denying that penises are meant to plant the seeds of life. But at the same time, if one of the many billions of penises in existence needs to be abolished so the rest of them can continue their pollination then that is a small sacrifice to pay. We are talking one dick in billions. And a small one at that I hear."

Thelma's sermon was not the most passionate piece of prose I had ever heard, but her math certainly made our potential plan seem a lot less sinister. She then changed the subject and asked,

"Are we allowed to eat on this stuff? I'm getting hungry."

Snopes became consumed with his new investigation. It was more than the revitalization of his passion; the case was so bizarre he was hooked on the novelty. It did not take him long to notice two of the vanishing penis events took place across the street from each other, so he interviewed those two victims. It was brought to his attention that right before the incident occurred they both came face to face with a man of my description. Upon questioning the penisless guy in the hospital, who would answer anything if it would lead to the return of his privates, he claimed there was a face to face, but hard to describe since I was wearing a mop hat at the time. Snopes created a wall map in his study showing the location of the three events. At the diner I was a customer, at Flimsy Fork I was a delivery guy, and at the march I was a protestor. He focused on the Flimsy Fork/Diner dynamic since they were so close and happened on different days.

The sketch-art Snopes was working with based on my description, fortunately resembled George Clooney. Not that I am as handsome as George, but we have some similar features. This was a lucky break for me because anyone he showed it to immediately laughed, and asked if Clooney was a suspect. It hadn't occurred to us yet but if Norman was seen at the site of any future penis event it would be possible to cross reference him with the Flimsy Fork incident, and narrow in on my identity. For this reason we were lucky it was just Thelma and me who flew to Kentucky to attend the Frumpf rally where it might be possible for me to look into the president's eyes without being noticed.

Like a thin plot from a porn film, the motel where we had booked two rooms only had one room available when we arrived. It had a queen bed that Thelma and I would have to share that night unless I slept on the floor. When we checked in, we didn't spend much time addressing the issue, and just focused on getting rid of our jitters, and heading to the afternoon Frumpf rally.

The stadium was buzzing. A bizarre array of Frumpf fanatics carried signs with inane slogans supporting his existence. Swastikas, skull and cross bones, and a litany of other evil, iconic references graced the promotional paraphernalia. To not appear out of place I wore a Harley Davidson t-shirt with the sleeves cut off, and Thelma donned a *Quik-Mart* baseball cap. The vibe upon entering the arena was thick with dissension. If disillusionment were smoke, we would have all died from asphyxiation. Two plump, braless, tank-topped septuagenarians were the epitome of the crowd. Their comments reeked of right-wing talk radio, and one of the shirts had an arrow pointing towards her crotch with the slogan; *grab me here*. We had to make our way close enough to the stage to be able to make eye contact with Frumpf. Thelma took on a persona that allowed us to snake right through the horde. She would give kudos to the slogans, and complimented the most hideous outfitted people on their threads. We eventually found two seats in the tenth row. I had once read that feature films were made to be seen from that row, so I relied on the only conventional wisdom I knew to choose our position. Being among this clueless crowd caused me to contemplate canceling our blitz, and letting the whole world self-destruct. It's one thing to read about the nature of Frumpf's rally supporters, but to be surrounded by them in the thousands was like being submerged in sludge. I'm sure there were many followers with sense and dignity, but after rubbing shoulders with the likes of these folks I couldn't wait to be done with this deed, and hit the motel shower to decontaminate.

Sitting through the array of propagandized speeches designed to augment the stature of Frumpf's appearance was torturous. I wanted to make all of their penises disappear, even the women's whose ideology was so inhumane I imagined they might have been packing one under their skirts. It shocks me why even one woman on the planet would promote allowing men to have control over their bodies and rights. Political pundits insist these people are brainwashed, but after hearing them speak there is obviously nothing clean about their thoughts. It should be called brain-dirtying. The final speaker was now listing Frumpf's *trumped up* accomplishments, all of which were really due to the providence of the previous president. The energy in the crowd kept building, and when he finally took the stage the bozo base gave Frumpf a rock star's welcome.

I was now unduly motivated to slay the dragon, and do to the president what has been done throughout history to make male slaves more compliant, and to reduce the despicable hunger of sex offenders. But I was about to take it to the extreme. Not just a castration, but a complete obliteration of presidential penishood. As I awkwardly tried to catch his eye I noticed that someone to the left of me appeared to be pulling a pistol out of his jacket pocket. As the gunman reached up to take aim at Frumpf, my humane instincts took over and I tackled him. The commotion had security on us instantly, and my ultimate target was quickly escorted off of the stage.

Thelma and I made it back to our motel room but were followed by the eager press. She would occasionally peek outside the curtains, and inform me the media was still gathered around like hungry wolves. How did this happen? I wasn't supposed to save his fucking life; I was supposed to make it miserable. Thelma suggested I answer a few questions to make the reporters go away. The last thing I wanted was to be on national television for saving Frumpf's life. The thought of having all of those wretched souls revering me for rescuing their golden calf made my stomach turn. Thelma finally convinced me to say something to make the looming circus disappear. I put on sunglasses and her baseball cap to be as incognito as possible. When I opened the motel room door the cameras loomed closer, and the verbal firing line began.

"How does it feel to be the hero who risked his life for the president?"

"I didn't risk my life," I insisted. "I followed my instinct as anyone would have done."

"Are you looking forward to meeting President Frumpf?"

At that moment it occurred to me I could now actually garner a face-to-face meeting with the prick. There would be no doubt I was the culprit, but I could be sure to get the deed done. Anything would be better than to be seen as his savior.

"There has been no mention of that," I replied. "Now my wife is feeling ill, so I would appreciate it if you would all let us be in peace. Thank you." I concluded.

Later that evening the commotion had finally died down. We were visited by White House security to give a statement of events and invited to meet President Frumpf. I graciously turned them down, again using the excuse that my wife was not feeling well, suggesting we would have to meet him another time. They offered to send over Frumpf's accompanying physician to check her out, but I assured him it was just too much excitement for one day.

So much had gone on we hadn't had time to sort out the sleeping arrangement. Thelma was lying back on her half talking to Norman on the phone about the day's events; he had seen my heroics on the news. I needed to take a load off, so I just plopped down next to her while she chatted. When her phone conversation ended, Thelma asked how I was doing. I told her I could use a drink. We raided the mini-bar and began to concoct odd cocktails with names we made up to signify our situation. There were the vodka and OJ, which we called the *Frumpf Screwer,* and the tequila and pineapple juice now called the *Penis Colada*.

My now famous tackle of the Frumpf assailant was repeatedly broadcast on the news. Thank god we were in Kentucky instead of New York where the media would be even more relentless in obtaining sound bites. Intoxication became obvious when we started screaming obscenities at the reporters on the TV. In the dim light of the television screen, with the hocus pocus of delinquent Jose Cuervo; Thelma exhibited a sexiness I hadn't noticed before. Out of respect for Norman, I tried to ignore the premise as Thelma muted the sound and stared into my eyes. She maintained I was looking at her as if I wanted to make her penis disappear. Through my mouth, Jose Cuervo told her that the reality was I was hoping to make mine temporarily vanish. She warned me she gets really hot when there is penis talk, and grabbed one of the bed pillows to cover her torso. I offered to leave until the heat died down. She ignored my offer as she commenced using the pillow to mimic being humped. Thelma was suddenly on fire and began to do things that would make any man jealous of that pillow. She insisted I watch and encouraged me to play with myself to deal with the stimulation. As if it was a logical command, I complied and found myself masturbating to Thelma feigning sex with the lucky cushion. The sight of me jerking off enhanced her lust, inspiring her to remove her shirt and bra, and caress her very full breasts with her hands. I continued to stroke with complete abandon, which made her hotter. She slithered out of her skirt and panties continuing to rub the pillow against her body like she was having sex. My hard-on felt like it was hot steel as she moaned in orgasmic ecstasy. As her breathing began to calm, she looked over at me continuing to stroke myself. What happened next I could neither endorse, nor resist, as she straddled me, and began to slide up and down with her breasts rubbing against my face. Out of guilt I made a feeble attempt to protest, but she put her finger to my lips and claimed Norman would not understand the naked pillow part so we might as well go all the way. The whole night became a sex fest of every maneuver imaginable. Thelma initiated it all as if this was her one free chance to experience something different than the paltry petting she was used to. When we were done, drained of our energy and juices, she looked into my eyes, and said,

"No reason for guilty, in my mind I just fucked George Clooney and what woman wouldn't?"

Morning was fuzzy. I awoke next to naked Thelma whose hand was on my thigh as she snored away. As I tried to slither out of bed, she awoke. She smiled as she moved her hand a little higher up until she eventually grasped my morning wood.

"Quite a night," she said without softening her grip.

"You and George certainly went at it," I responded.

"You think George likes it in the morning," she asked, now increasing the pressure of her grasp.

At this point, I could no longer look to Jose Cuervo, Johnnie Walker, Jim Beam, or any of the other guys I could blame for the previous night's adulterous tryst. I was now aware of my senses, but the touch of her hand on my cock went straight to my lenient, decision-making committee. A combination of my hesitation to answer and an obvious penile region pulsation made Thelma take that as a yes. She pulled the blanket down with her other hand exposing my erection, and began to move her mouth in its direction. As her lips were close enough for me to feel the heat of her breath there was a loud, intrusive knock on the motel room door that instantly snapped us out of our imminent debauchery.

I was now facing a few men in matching suits and could see a bunch of cliché black cars in the background. Frumpf's agents insisted we accompany them to Air Force One and added that our motel bill would be paid for. Wait till they get the mini-bar tab, I thought. After negotiating a few minutes for us to shower and pack, Thelma and I were in the back seat of a large SUV heading to Frumpf's plane. Thelma called Norman to explain we were heading to

Washington and promised she would let him know what out itinerary was as soon as we knew. Although everything was happening fast, and being on our way to meet Frumpf was daunting, my mind was still on Thelma's warm lips that minutes ago were about to devour me into oblivion.

Upon arriving at the tarmac, we caught a gawker's glance of Frumpf boarding Air Force One. Seeing the words United States of America written across the fuselage instantly made our mission feel way too real. Richard J. Frumpf was different up close. At first glimpse his eyes were dead, lacking the presence you would expect from that of a world leader. His skin resembled a sun-bleached tangerine. The only lively feature was his hair, which held a web-like style all its own, seeming to have been colored by an experimental dye that hadn't quite yet been perfected. As he reached out to shake my hand, I noticed his hands were absurdly tiny, and not representative of power in the slightest way. He clamped both his hands around mine and pulled me toward him, in a way that felt more desperate than welcoming. His shake was off center and lasted way too long to feel comfortable. When he released, he just nodded his head at Thelma as if she was inconsequential. Even through his vapid eyes, I could tell he was wondering why a young, good-looking guy like myself didn't have a younger wife. He imported First Lady Teresa when she was 18, after discovering her modeling at a Hungarian fashion event. His dreadful pickup line was that he was almost Hungarian, just the first four letters worth. I was about to change that.

It would soon have to come out that I was not married to Thelma, and we were just on a trip together. The only story I could think of was we were both avid Frumpf supporters not wanting to miss the rally her husband couldn't attend because of work. Hopefully, my explanation wouldn't have to go as far as why we were sharing a one bed room, even though there was a paper trail proving it was not our intention. Frumpf told me he appreciated my heroism in attempting to save his life but arrogantly added that the freak with the gun probably would have missed anyway. I appreciated that he was tempering my participation in the rescue, but could not ignore the fact the son-of-a-bitch was watering down the event, so he wasn't beholden to anyone, or perceived as weak. I wasn't even curious about the assailant as I assumed over half the country wanted Frumpf dead.

He then asked how I would like to be honored and rewarded for what I did. Without missing a beat, I told him a couple of hot coffees and breakfast for two would be more than enough. Frumpf grinned where one would expect a laugh, and then bragged that his accompanying private chef made the best breakfast on the planet.

I was not expecting white shag carpeting to be covering the floor of the dining compartment. Frumpf claimed it reminded him of his daughter, as this was the floor covering of her bedroom as a child. Thelma rolled her eyes as if to say "What a perv." Fortunately, Frumpf didn't notice. When our cappuccinos arrived, the president told us to be careful not to spill because coffee can stain the rug. He added that for this reason red wine is not even allowed on the plane. The man's small-minded personality caused me to dislike him even more than I already did. Here he was the most powerful entity in the world, ready to drop blood-drenching bombs on innocent people, yet worried about a burgundy mishap. So here I was, point blank with the man I have been planning to target for weeks. All I had to do was look into his soulless eyes with intention, and bingo, my mission would be easily accomplished. As usual of late, Thelma picked up on my thoughts, causing her to casually nod her head to signify this was not yet the right moment.

*18

Dinner for three was set to launch at the Snopes household. CNN was on in the background. The talking heads argued about who was the real hero; the guy who wanted to shoot Frumpf, or me. The dialogue was heated as one of the guest speakers, a Hispanic woman whose husband was deported after 14 years paying taxes in the states, claimed the country would welcome the opportunity to mourn Frumpf's demise.

"He is ill...illogical, illiterate, and illegitimate." she ranted.

When the doorbell rang, Snopes hurried over to welcome his daughter and her "partner" Angela. After the formalities, they sat around the dining room table. Snopes cracked a bottle of white wine and poured everyone a glass. As he held up his drink for a toast, Angela seized the spiel,

"To family."

They clinked their glasses in solidarity.

*19

Perched on an antique loveseat facing a matching sofa across from where I am resting, Thelma surveyed the surrounding opulence of the Lincoln bedroom. She recited a list of past guests that read like a who's who of global celebrity. Apparently, previous administrations used the bedroom as a way to raise funds. Oddly, the one person that never slept in the bedroom was Lincoln himself, as he had used it as an office. As historically awesome as it all seemed, I said I needed to inform our hosts that Thelma wasn't my wife, and get a separate room. I feared there was no way we would be able to keep this from Norman, which meant we would be screwed. Thelma congratulated me on my choice of words but assured me our hosts already know everything about us. She declared it is not like they invite complete strangers to sleep in the White House. She said they probably already knew our life history, but ventured to allege Frumpf is such a devious fuck he is probably living vicariously through what he saw as our secret affair. I remind her that our whole conversation is probably being recorded, and still insisted we ask for separate rooms. Thelma wasn't concerned at all, and could not believe this was my focus when we were about to perform my special magic act to save the world.

 A female valet arrived at the room with formal wear for us both. She informed us someone would escort us to the dining room in two hours at 6:30 prompt. I was overwhelmed by the situation, failing to express our lodging dilemma to her. Thelma was completely entranced in the whole endeavor. As she set her evening gown out on the bed to admire it, I shook my head in acknowledgment that we were treading in shark-infested waters.

*20

One bottle of wine sat empty and the second one half full. The chicken had been consumed, and Ella was sidled closer to Angela. Ella encouraged her dad to tell Angela what he's working on. He began to talk about his agricultural grafting experiments. Ella stopped him, telling him she meant the other thing, the vanishing penis investigation. Snopes asked Angela if she had read about the rash of incidences lately. She replied that sometimes she wished her penis would magically appear, soliciting major laughs from Ella, but catching Snopes off guard, as the comment taught him a bit more about the dynamics of his daughter's relationship than he cared to know at that moment. Angela claimed it was a gay thing to be investigating missing penises, causing Snopes to insist he didn't have a homosexual bone in his body. Angela rebutted that all men have that *bone,* provoking Ella to elbow her, reminding her that Snopes was her dad. Angela apologized, saying in her worldview men were overly obsessed about penis activity: where can they put it; how they can make it bigger; and how to ensure it worked. She said the recent stories in the tabloids were over-sensationalized paranoia from the male population. She hypothesized the fear of vanishing penises was the underlying motivation of the rank Republican Party to get behind Frumpf, the ultimate dick. Snopes laughed and agreed she was not wrong about the last part, which lightened the mood at the table.

The White House ballroom was buzzing with familiar faces; senators, the press secretary, cabinet members, Frumpf's family; including his wife Teresa and daughter Valina, both stunning in their evening gowns. Even Frumpf had the semblance of a glow in his tuxedo. They were all gathered closely as if formal state dinner protocol was mitigated to hold an unconventional surprise party for an awaited recipient.

When Thelma and I were escorted into the room, we were greeted by thunderous applause. Valina approached us, and graciously hugged us individually, thanking us for saving her father's life. One by one we were greeted and congratulated by people we both despised due to their reputation of conservative, corrupt, racist policies. How bizarre is life that a mission to take down Frumpf led to him honoring us with a ballyhooed reception? I wondered if this was the universe's way of preventing us from doing the wrong thing. As the champagne flowed, and the hors d'oeuvres flourished, Thelma played the part well. First displayed by her Frumpf rally demeanor, it was obvious she had some advanced chameleonic personality traits. I was still harboring guilt for not only spending the previous night in complete sexual abandon with Norman's wife, but here I was now masquerading as her husband at a White House gala event. To make matters worse, the more champagne Thelma drank, the more I sensed a submissive glance that warned me she was hoping to later show Lincoln what handling a log was all about.

Flashing on the fate of Lincoln reminded me of my mission. It was time to do my duty. Not only would I save the world from this degenerate, but it would also give me the perfect excuse in Norman's eyes as to why I continued the marital charade with Thelma. I looked over at my executive target that embodied complete gluttony as he stuffed his fat face with a third helping of the dinner's main course.

*22

Angela was in the cab as Ella was saying goodnight to her dad. She apologized for Angela's outspoken opinions, but claimed that was one of the things she loved about her. She thanked him for being such a gracious host and said they would have him over to their place soon. They hugged, she got into the taxi, and Snopes waved as it pulled away. He then walked around the garage to the backyard where there was a large greenhouse. He entered and turned on the light exposing a brigade of starter-plants in a variety of plastic containers. He approached one plant that was obviously more prominent than the rest. He gave it a tiny bit of water and wished it goodnight.

Dessert plates were arriving with chronological precision. Frumpf eyed the chocolate delicacy like a salivating mutt. He sat at the head of the table with me, the guest of honor, seated directly to his right. I kept wondering about the best time to annihilate the bastard, but I didn't feel the moment was yet perfect to pull the trigger. Admittedly, I was terrified. Frumpf stood up to give a speech. He told everyone that heroes like me are what true patriotism was about, and embarrassingly compared me to his voters that bravely elected him into office. I wanted to puke, but I had to admit that the duck they served for dinner was worthy of keeping down. He then claimed although there were those who didn't understand his greatness, the whole nation would eventually celebrate his existence, or **he would be struck by lightening at that very moment**.

I was unsure if it was the word lightening or the thunder in Thelma's eyes that sanctioned the moment, but I knew it was show time. The curtains had opened at the figurative Ford Theater, and it was now or never. As Frumpf, the president of the United States of America, glanced over at me in admiration, I looked back with venom-loaded eyes that held enough disrespect to evaporate his being even without my special gift. His pupils were about to meet the ultimate teacher, and unfortunately for him learn the hard way what happens when self-interest overrules global prosperity. Instead of fear, I felt gallant as I stared right into the paragon of evil in its most unsettling form, causing my emasculating power to flow into Frumpf's peepers like a laser.

In the midst of the sycophants applauding his vainglorious oration, his victorious demeanor turned to that of concern as he suddenly felt something strange in his groin. Frumpf rushed away from the table without a word, exiting the ballroom. A few seconds later, Richard J. Frumpf's scream of horror shook the presidential portraits hanging on the White House walls.

Thelma and I were quickly escorted back to the Lincoln bedroom. They instructed us to remain there as a security measure since there was a classified situation in progress. "Ha," I thought, "a missing penis is now classified information." My act of humanitarian vengeance was right alongside Iran-Contra, Watergate, and even Monica's blowjob. Damn, just when I had my thoughts completely on political history the Monica reference brought to mind I was again about to sleep in the same bed as the pillow monster. It was unlikely with all the commotion that we would partake in a remake of last night's event, but as I looked over at Thelma leaning against the headboard in her gorgeous designer evening gown that accentuated her breasts, I could tell she was intent on having me visit, excuse the expression, her oval office.

Norman, Norman, Norman. Why does it seem like I am the only one of us thinking about you at all? Your wife is acting like a teenager whose parents are away on a trip. Norman, Norman, Norman. Does fucking her twice make our promiscuous liaison doubly wrong? As if she again knows what I am thinking, Thelma takes hold of one of the pillows and puts it on her lap. Norman, Norman, Norman. If we act too sterile, we might become suspects in Frumpf's dilemma, and be incarcerated for life. Norman, Norman. Maybe the best thing to do is have amazing sex so in case they are listening it seems like we have nothing to hide. Norman, Norman. This may be the last night of sex in my whole life if you don't count the kind of sex one has in prison. Although most inmates are evil enough for me to do away with their instrument of intrusion, I could only vanish one dick per day. Hard to stay ahead of that game, especially when I resemble George Clooney.

Thelma was now standing with her back to me unzipping her evening gown. Norman! As the top of the gown folded forward, she unlatched her bra and allowed it to fall to the floor exposing exquisite side boob. Norm! In an attempt to resist I thought about what would happen if Abe came home and caught us in his bedroom. Nor! Thelma was now completely naked under the lush blankets of the handsomely carved bed. With one finger she summoned me to forget that Norman exists.

On our way to the Airport, Frumpf's assistant Barbara apologized for the president's abrupt exit and unavailability, but assured us he would be in touch. She promised to make sure we received copies of the gala photos when they are printed and framed and handed us both an expensive black leather bag that included a 'Make America Great Again' baseball cap, as well as various items sporting the presidential seal. We were escorted through airport security right onto the plane where we would be flying First Class to JFK.

When we arrived in New York Norman was anxiously waiting at the baggage claim. Thelma acted happy to see him and seemed to possess zilch in the guilt department. I, on the other hand, had not only just pruned the president's privates, but on the same night re-deflowered Norman's wife in the very room of a much more honest Abe. Attempting to mask my inner turmoil I just handed Norman my gifted leather satchel with all the goodies and claimed it was a present for Norman from Frumpf himself, who at this moment would have been much better off had Norman been his guest. On the drive back to their home Norman had many questions. I allowed Thelma to do the talking, as she was carefree and full of polished responses. Fortunately, overcoming the assailant at the rally, and making Frumpf's dick disappear at the dinner, were the most compelling topics. Questions about the sleeping arrangement didn't come up at all so far. Thelma even chanced flaunting she got to sleep in the Lincoln bedroom while I was relegated an appropriate quarters named after John Wilkes Booth. I had to hand it to her, Thelma was very smooth.

Stressed beyond poise from the recent escapades, I ventured to lay low by visiting an old girlfriend, Lana Page in Woodstock. Lana reminded me of my mother in that she too saw herself as a shaman. She made a living teaching yoga and producing art designed to transform your energy field. She claimed to be able to see the hue of your aura, and use that information to balance your environment with what she called counter-colors. I figured my energy field probably needed the whole damn rainbow right about now. I could never survive like one of those Marvel Comic characters that are addicted to meddling with maniacs. Eradicating the president's penis was my swan song, and I am now retired. Lana's small log cabin is without TV, and the only sign of electronics is a lavender Bluetooth speaker that seeped gypsy jazz around the clock, and a small Ipad she mostly used to maintain her online art commerce. You would think that after my recent lodging, a log cabin would be the last place I would go to take my mind off of things, but the Lincoln reference didn't even occur to me until the day I left. Lana was apolitical and believed that the same way religion was the opiate of the masses, the media was the *meth* of society. Her presence alone alleviated a world of worry, a worry I wouldn't share so as not to drag her peaceful mind into my drama.

Occasionally the mere absence of sound can be deafening. The sound of silence coming from the West Wing was a suspicious scream. Snopes had heard the president might be dying of some illness; maybe even cancer, and that Frumpf's legion of liars was trying to keep it all under wraps. But when one of his FBI cohorts mentioned there was a rumor surfacing that Frumpf was having a severe problem with his penis, it captured Snopes' attention. Could it be possible? Did the George Clooney doppelganger manage to Siegfried the president's Roy? Certainly explains why no one was talking about it. Snopes reviewed news footage of Frumpf's recent public appearances, the most magnetizing of which was the attempted assassination. As he viewed the assailant being tackled, he froze the scene on a shot of my face. Zooming in for a closer look, he noticed that in a loose way I resembled George Clooney, but that didn't add up. Why would the penis bandit save the president's life only to decapitate his dick? He realized he wasn't even sure Frumpf's penis had been tampered with and decided he needed to seek definitive confirmation.

Obtaining an appointment to meet with Frumpf's Chief Of Staff required pulling strings. Snopes arrived at the White House armed with a file full of news clippings regarding the recent vanishing penis stories. After the preliminary introduction, Snopes placed the clips on the table without a word. He watched the chief's face for his reaction. The chief asked why Snopes was showing this to him. Snopes claimed he had been investigating these occurrences, and without stating his new suspicion asked if it was in the White House's interest to get to the bottom of it. The chief took the clippings with him and requested Snopes to wait. Snopes was sure he hit the nail on the head because the chief would have dismissed the whole thing instantly had there not been some interest in his knowledge.

A lone Secret Service agent returned to the room and escorted Snopes to another area of the White House. When Snopes realized he was being taken to an in-house medical facility, he pondered how much he would reveal to them. Although he recently assumed I might have something to do with all of this, he wasn't sure and did not want to dispel false allegations. When Snopes was finally facing Frumpf, he was impressed with all the high-tech medical equipment in existence to deal with a case of zero genitalia. Snopes was made aware this was strictly classified and confidential. He realized *he* was now under scrutiny for even being aware of the issue, but at this moment the primary concern to all, especially Frumpf, was how to get to the bottom of this, pun intended.

*25

My few days in Woodstock turned into a week of repose. I was stretched, cleansed, and had all of my chakras realigned. The Republicans should adopt Lana-care I thought, instead of their creepy attempt to pass worthless medical legislation. I told Lana I had to go back to the city to put some affairs in order, and threatened to return to continue our re-acquaintance, even though my mind was swarming with passionate panoramas of Thelma.

When I arrived at my apartment, the door was slightly ajar, so I entered cautiously. Sitting on my couch, manhandling one of my many crystals was a gent I have never seen before. He wasn't armed, and his comportment was non-imposing, so I simply asked what he was doing there. He introduced himself as Investigator Peter Snopes of the FBI, and he wanted to have a chat. I overlooked his shoddy entry behavior, as illegal as it was, and feigning ignorance I asked if this was about tackling the assailant at the Frumpf rally. Snopes smiled at my question then asked if I was a fan of magic. I said I was a bit fascinated with slight of hand, to which he replied,

"What about slight of something else?"

I wasn't certain he was referring to penises, but I could tell by the way he said "something else," that this conversation would be traveling in an unfortunate direction. Without offering him confirmation, Snopes asked me how I performed my feat. He said although he wasn't sure if my parlor trick could be considered a crime, or even provable for that matter, circumstantially he was intrigued. Choosing not to play dumb, I came clean and gave Snopes the full scoop, omitting the participation of Thelma, Norman, and anyone else that may have been privy to the operation. Snopes loved that he was sitting in the very place it all started and insisted I wasn't wrong in believing that I was doing the world a favor by neutering Frumpf. After ten minutes in Frumpf's presence, Snopes confessed he felt like cutting off his head. But what should he do with his new bundle of investigative gems, he wondered? He thought it was amusing that Handy Randy was only a test run, and was curious who was next on my hit list. I explained I had no desire to use the power ever again. Snopes said he was going to stew on all this for a while, and suggested I remained in the vicinity.

When I arrived at Thelma and Norman's home to say goodbye, and give them a heads up on the Snopes dope, Norman was still at work. I assured Thelma I kept them out of the loop. I reached into my pocket, handed her one of my mom's larger crystals as a gift, and disclosed that our time together was nothing short of unforgettable. I said that I hoped the global effects of our Frumpf endeavor would wind up being well worth our efforts. She teased that it was already well worth hers, and asked where I was going. I said that due to the circumstances of being investigated it would be better if she were unaware. We hugged tightly; she hugged tighter and said she would miss me. My self-imprisoned psyche wanted to break out and put all feelings on the table, but I was afraid she would share things I wasn't ready to hear or know how to handle. As I exited her home I was sure of one thing; we would surely cross paths again soon.

*26

One amazing presidential perk was having access to absolutely everything, which is how Frumpf already had prosthetic private parts fitted to his crotch that attached to the catheter, so he was able to mimic taking a leak. Mr. Ego of course had them make the prosthetics larger than his former privates. His medical advisors felt it would be psychologically beneficial for him to feel like his penis was still intact, and keep his mood emotionally balanced, a major feat since he wasn't that way to begin with. There were meetings behind closed doors of those Republicans in the know about how to move forward with a dickless commander in chief. They knew they couldn't release the truth to the public, as the threat that there was someone out there that could decimate your dick could cause major panic. They also didn't believe Frumpf would be able to weather the ridicule, as dick jokes, the easiest jokes in the world, would run rampant. For now, it was decided to keep the ordeal secret until further notice. It wasn't long before Frumpf's disposition made him crankier, which darkly reflected in his executive orders and decisions. He was in an all-out war against anyone that might be experiencing joy. He kept introducing legislation that would weaken the public's privacy, and undo civil rights.

All footage of Frumpf in the media was of him sitting behind his desk. Though that isn't what made the public suspicious that something was wrong, it was that he was no longer playing golf. After years of ridiculing previous presidents for spending time on the greens, Frumpf played every weekend at his private course costing the taxpayers millions of dollars. Some were so angry they renamed the ultimate shot after him calling it an *AssHole in one*. The populous voiced extreme dissension regarding his game, but seeing him suddenly stop raised a big red flag. Rumors began to leak online and theories engaged; Parkinson's, anxiety disorders, increased brain damage, but no one guessed the real problem, yet.

Delving deep into the science was all Snopes could do at this point. He interviewed anatomy professors, acupuncturists', black magic practitioners, yogis, and anyone else that had something to do with alternative theories regarding anatomy. He wondered if the magic only worked on evil people, what if they stopped being evil? He returned to my apartment to discuss the theory further but found it vacated. I had taken my belongings, including my mother's crystal collection, and moved to Woodstock to be with Lana. Snopes tried my cell, but it went straight to voicemail. He left many messages claiming it was essential he speak with me ASAP.

There were a few reasons Lana and I separated back in the day. I felt she was too strict and anal about the necessity to disconnect from all media and airwave signals. Every time I bit into a sandwich she lectured me on the perils of wheat. Our butter had to be clarified along with a litany of house rules I had trouble following. Since then she has lightened up, and will even watch a film online if she deemed it had a positive message. Forget screening films like *Fast and Furious,* as *Slow and Happy* is her coveted underlining theme. I needed to believe I was ready to try again, and distance my heart from another man's wife. Lana was more than willing to indulge my stated desire to reconnect in a more enlightened way. She designed each day to involve an experience that would enhance our senses. She whipped up healthy culinary treats that woke up taste buds I didn't know existed. We swam in a local river that was just cold enough to shake up our spirits, and she showed me how to separate the various sounds of the flow so it would take me to a meditative state of consciousness. All Lana's yoga students were gorgeous-young-flexible-goddess types that had a crush on her. What I lack as a yogini I make up for in the way I can stretch my imagination. It is hard for me to determine if I was taking to this lifestyle because I honestly loved it, or was using it as an escape like a *consciousness protection program.* I hadn't checked my messages in a while, but felt I needed to monitor the news occasionally for any pertinent Frumpf revelations.

*27

It was a snap for Snopes to trace down Thelma, my obvious partner in crime during the whole White House scenario. He did his homework though and believed he was holding a valuable interrogation card. Even without his credentials, Thelma would have invited him in, as she is the consummate hostess, and would make coffee for a burglar if they had the time. Seated at the kitchen table, Snopes made it clear he was not trying to involve her in unnecessary drama, and just needed help contacting me. Thelma insisted I wouldn't share my whereabouts, and apologized that she couldn't help. Snopes wondered aloud if Norman was privy to the dynamics of our recent excursion. Without missing a beat Thelma assured him that if she knew where I was his blackmail might have been effective, but she didn't, so he was milking a dry cow. She offered him some of her special gefilte fish without telling him how special it really was. When Snopes asked for seconds, Thelma suggested he savor the flavor and avoided telling him why she wouldn't comply. She was not the type to spike someone without their knowledge or consent, but there was something about Snopes' attempt to extort an admission that caused her to break the rules. She wasn't poisoning him; he would just get very stoned. Wrapping up the interview, Snopes asked Thelma how much she knew about the magic part of my power. He even inquired about what she thought would happen if the victim changed their ways, and was no longer evil. She had no idea but added if his hope was for Frumpf to change, he had a better chance of rerouting the Rio Grande.

*28

Asserting Frumpf was beginning to lose it was like stating the polar icecaps were starting to melt. It was obvious to the public from the beginning that his feeble mind was a few students short of an electoral college, but recent events have pushed any semblance of sanity even further towards the asylum. The idea he would never have a dick again was more than he could handle. First lady Teresa on the other hand, was secretly thrilled about his missing anatomy, as she only married him for his opulence, and abhorred having sex with him at all. It was like being fucked by a portly penguin, she thought. He awkwardly offered to satisfy her with his prosthetic dick, but she claimed she would wait for the real thing to return, which she hoped never would. Teresa wasn't a bad egg, she was gorgeous, and assumed her beauty had cashed in on the dream until she realized she was married to the ultimate nightmare. Frumpf was so narcissistic he would often ignore her existence, and even walked ahead with people while she lagged behind on her own. Many men would have licked the ground Teresa walked on, but Frumpf saw her as not only a trophy, but as an accessory whose only task was to satisfy his whims and make him look prominent. She had wanted out of the marriage for years but was hoping that instead of divorce the daily Prozac/Viagra/Statin combo would cause him to kick the gilded bucket. She had no idea he would ever become president, and backing out now was more complicated.

29

His greenhouse had become a funhouse as Snopes tended to the soil while expounding on the meaning of plant-life to his seedlings.

"I sympathize with you about how hard it must be to try and grow healthy knowing the better you look, the greater your chances are of being devoured. I feel for you, I really do. But you all need to realize how amazing you are. You can prevent cancer; I can't do that," he claimed.

Snopes was feeling the effects of Thelma's gefilte fish and was a better man for it. He didn't even question why he was loaded, and just embraced it. As he pranced around, he heard his doorbell faintly ringing, but thought it was his imagination. Then through the frosted glass of the greenhouse, he saw a shadow moving toward him. He stood silent for a moment as the ensuing figure revealed itself at the entrance to be Inspector Lice. The odd chance Lice would show up at Snopes' home in the evening caused him laughter. When Lice asked what was so funny, the seriousness of Lice's demeanor caused Snopes to laugh more. When he regained his composure, Snopes introduced his friend to his plants,

"Plants, Lice, Lice, plants," he humorously stated.

Lice said he had some serious issues to discuss, and suggested relocating to the main house. Snopes claimed he first had to pee in the plant bucket, inviting Lice to do the same if he had to go. Lice declined, and as Snopes urinated in the pail, he declared that urine was one of the best-kept horticultural secrets because if the American public knew their veggies were human pee-fortified they wouldn't eat them. In the living room, over Scotch, Lice revealed the White House had asked the FBI to check into what Snopes was up to. They were concerned he had not been totally upfront with them. Snopes asked Lice if he was aware of the current dilemma. Lice claimed the whole bureau knows about Frumpf's missing dick and admitted he thought it pretty suspicious that Snopes was investigating the phenomenon way before it was a presidential issue. Snopes attempted to lighten the mood by asking Lice if he would have ever believed one day they would be discussing the ramifications of the president's missing dick. Lice smiled for a second but said Snopes needed to understand the gravity of the situation. He underlined that the White House is now relying on Snopes to fix it, or he may go down as a suspect.

"Go down?" Snopes asked. "Unless I fix it there will be no going down."

Lice asked if Snopes was on something, to which Snopes replied that he honestly wasn't sure. He claimed he might have been spiked, because he was feeling looser than usual, and everything seemed beautiful.

"Everything but you Licey," he mocked.

Lice didn't know what to make of it all and insisted Snopes get his act together so he could put the problem to rest.

*30

While Lana was on a day hike with her girlfriends, I finally decided to check my messages. There were ten from Snopes, and a few from Thelma telling me I needed to contact him. He was honestly the last person I wanted to speak with because I was sure it would drag me back to a state of mind I was happy to have jettisoned. But when I listened to the message threatening if I didn't call him back soon he was going to have words with Norman, I decided it was time to check in.

Snopes claimed we needed a face to face, and arranged a meeting in a small café in the city for the next day. I told Lana I had some personal business to take care of and would be back in the evening. She made me a thermos of Mu tea, instructing me to sip on it throughout the day to stay calm. When I entered the café, I spotted Snopes seated in the corner drinking coffee. He was overly friendly and took me off guard. I couldn't be sure it wasn't my Woodstock consciousness that made everything appear disarming, but he seemed genuinely happy to see me. The first question out of his mouth was not what I expected. He inquired if I had ever tried Thelma's gefilte fish. Without waiting for an answer, he stated it was quite magnificent. He told me not to worry about his Norman threat, saying he was just desperate to hear from me. He explained the White House and FBI were breathing down his neck, and if someone didn't come up with a remedy for Frumpf soon all hell would break loose. I empathized with his situation but claimed there was nothing I could do or undo for that matter. Snopes brought up his *stop being evil* theory and wondered if it could reverse the effects. He claimed although we all wanted Frumpf ousted, if this situation stopped him from being wicked and corrupt maybe we could put up with him until the next election without any major concerns. He shared Thelma's Rio Grande retort regarding the unlikelihood of Frumpf changing, which made me miss her even more than I already did. He said if nothing else works we could furnish the prez with a four-year supply of her Gefilte Fish. As I pondered it all, I opened the thermos, and took a sip to relax my thoughts. I told Snopes it was a special Mu tea concoction given to me by an old friend.

The idea a scoundrel might regain his privates upon becoming genuinely benevolent was not outside the realm of possibility, but there was nothing to back up the theory but conventional logic. The reason it was unlikely was that a drastic personality shift from someone as deeply disturbed as Frumpf was so improbable it was not even worth considering. I told Snopes that if Frumpf's motivation to change was an effort to get his dick back then that in itself would probably negate all reversal possibilities. He asked again if there was any other way I could think of that was even remotely possible. I reiterated I was in no way a master of my magic, and unless Frumpf suddenly became someone to respect I wouldn't even spend a second trying to reverse the curse. Snopes then asked the million-dollar question of what I would do if they incarcerate Thelma or me until I resolve it. I thought about it for a second and took another big sip of Mu tea.

I called Thelma to check how she was holding up. She's the queen of carrying on as if nothing was wrong, but I worried she was keeping it all inside. She requested I stop by. When I arrived at the house, she greeted me wearing a thick terry cloth robe, and gave me a big hug. We sat on the living room couch laughing about how stoned Snopes said he got, and that he even asked if there was a way he could get more. I shared the recent White House gossip Snopes had clued me in about. Thelma claimed no one said saving the world would be without issues. As we spoke, her robe kept loosening little by little, and she was very distracted. Then in the middle of our conversation, she stood up and opened it all the way to reveal some risqué lingerie. She asked me what I thought, as the robe dropped to the ground freeing her to twirl around so I could get a 360. I told her even if I gave in to the urges we both knew existed, I could never do it right there in Norman's home. My statement didn't stop her from attempting to entice me further. As I weakened with contemplation, a car pulled into the driveway. Norman was home. Norman, Norman, Norman. Thelma quickly rushed upstairs leaving me to greet her unsuspecting husband. He was glad to see me, and I wished the feeling had been mutual. He shared that the FBI had been at Flimsy Fork interviewing everyone separately, especially Handy Randy who they questioned for over an hour. Norman said they wanted to know why his wife and I traveled together to Kentucky and the White House as a married couple. When I asked him how he responded, Norman said he told them the truth; he wasn't aware this was the case. I couldn't exactly read his attitude, but it was a cross between sad and confused. He then asked me point blank why we were traveling as if we were married. Oh how I wished Thelma were the one facing this firing line because I was sure I was about to symbolically neuter Norman. As I was about to give it my best shot, Thelma appeared and said,

"Honey, the truth is so boring I feel like making something up just for fun. We were heading to castrate Frumpf. After Sheldon so foolishly saved the asshole's life, the Feds wanted to whisk us away into their vehicle. Sheldon was so overwhelmed by it all that he used me as an excuse by informing them that his wife was feeling ill. At that point, we had to go along with the charade."

Norman chewed on that for a minute and asked,

"So how did you explain that you were sleeping in different rooms?"

I knew this question would eventually rear its ugly head. I had no worthy response, and as if we were both part of the inquisition, Norman and I looked at Thelma for an answer. She went on,

"So there we are in the Lincoln Bedroom discussing how we are going to tell them we need separate rooms when an aid drops by delivering formalwear for our evening gala attire. We decided we would have dinner, make Frumpf's penis vanish, then concoct some excuse about my illness necessitating me sleeping alone that night."

Norman jumped in, and asked why we needed to wait till after dinner instead of handling it immediately?

Thelma answered,

"Darling, we were about to commit a form of treason, and did not want to create any suspicion. Asking for different rooms may have seemed awkward. After the big event, we were brought back to the Lincoln Bedroom and told we were basically under lockdown due to a classified situation. So we slept together."

Both Norman and I appeared shocked at her admission. Norman looked at her perplexed, and then looked at me with daggers. She then added,

"Yes Norman, the Lincoln bed is large, and for the most part we were up all night freaked out about what just happened. I finally fell asleep with my clothes on at 5 A.M., two hours after snore-face over here went unconscious. There was nothing we could do, and who cares? You're my husband, not him."

Somehow her quasi-honest narrative hit home with Norman. I joked she could have left the snoring part out, but she wasn't done. As his final question Norman asked why she had told him I slept in the John Wilkes Booth room, to which she replied,

"It was a metaphor Norman, if you had to put up with that obnoxious snoring, you would have thought about assassination as well."

Wow, what a performance. Suddenly I wished it were possible to show my appreciation by giving her lingerie the full attention is deserved.

*31

Idsel Cohen was not just any therapist because he currently spends two hours every week listening to the trials and tribulations of Valina Frumpf. Being raised by Richard J. Frumpf was ripe with hurdles, even though Valina was spoiled to the point of absurdum. Not unlike the suspicious public, Valina herself wondered if her dad had been inappropriate at times during her upbringing, and often shared past scenarios with the doc to see if he thought Frumpf's behavior improper. It's a fine line to walk being the therapist of the president's daughter. If he did conceive that the president had acted with perversion, was it okay to let on? What if she went to Frumpf, and claimed her shrink said he is a perv? It is not the place of the therapist to even make such a judgment, but even if he was just being empathetic to Valina's disclosures, she could misconstrue it as confirmation her dad was a deviant.

On this particular day, Valina's psyche was like a leaky faucet about to burst. She claimed to now be holding too many governmental secrets due to her dad confiding in her about everything from war to wages. She understood it was hard to find someone to trust in government, so she indulged her dad as much as time would allow. She claimed there was one thing weighing on her more than anything, and she needed to share it. Idsel expressed that one of the reasons he was there was so she had an outlet she could confide in. With that concept in mind, she looked him in the eyes and said,

"My dad's penis is missing!"

Idsel was a veteran of the field. He was top in his class at Harvard and had been practicing for almost 30 years. To this day he had never heard anything as hard to process as Valina's statement.

"By missing, you mean in your life?" He asked.

Valina maintained her serious rapport and with an increased timbre said,

"No, it has completely vanished. My dad, the president of the USA, no longer has private parts and I don't know what to do!"

As she broke down in tears, the doc was unsure of how to handle this. Was she suffering from delusions? Was this a reaction to some childhood molestation that has manifested in her belief her dad is now dickless? Any sensible person knows a penis just doesn't disappear. Sure it shrinks or maintains unwanted flaccidity, and if lucky it occasionally vanishes within the confines of a welcoming vagina, but vaporizing into thin air without notice is what most would consider impossible. Idsel was witnessing Valina's implosion and decided to remain silent to see where it would go.

Florence Cohen collected Bakelite trinkets from the 1940s. She also collected original fiesta ware and antique Bauer plates. She gave up her own therapy practice years ago after suffering from a depression she believed was brought on by listening to everyone's sad crap on a regular basis. Let's face it, people don't visit their shrink to share good news, which makes a therapist a virtual verbal garbage dump. Some, like Idsel, can find the joy in alleviating the angst in others, but Florence had enough, and since her husband Idsel was bringing in plenty of dough she decided to flit around D.C. collecting things. Given that Florence had been a licensed shrink, and Idsel trusted her with his life, he decided to share with her Valina's declaration that Frumpf's penis was missing. Much to Idsel's surprise, instead of being shocked, Florence stated if there is a God the best thing he could do to that perverted, sexist, narcissist, was castration. Still, when Idsel went into the details Valina eventually shared about the situation, Florence became equally intrigued. So fascinated she was with this novelty of the story that she decided to do a "promise not to tell" with her sister Rose, who did not quite have the same code of ethics.

32

The vanishing penis caper had Snopes at a standstill. He now knew who'd done it, why he did it, and that its reversal was most likely undoable. He didn't want to turn me in, nor did he want to be the one to let Frumpf know that he would probably be dickless for the rest of his life. The hard truth about Frumpf's evilness was that he kept adding on to it instead of relinquishing it. Snopes debated about whether or not to share his theory about reversing the evil since not only was it unproven, but also unlikely it could occur. As he perused the internet for any mention of vanishing penises, something he did daily, he came across a couple of twitter posts that claimed the president was the latest victim of disappearing penis syndrome. Although he was surprised to see it was beginning to surface, he wrote it off as possible conspiratorial nonsense. *Then the world changed.* When Snopes was at the market buying his regular barbecue chicken, he saw the front page of all the tabloids had a story claiming Frumpf was dickless. It didn't take long before it caught on, and the Internet was on fire with jokes and stories about the president's administration being *understaffed*. The fact Frumpf's first name was Richard, which is usually abbreviated by calling someone Dick, did not help. Snopes decided he had better come up with a possible solution, even if it was farfetched, to help cushion the impact of the unmerciful ridicule Frumpf would receive. He wasn't empathetic, just worried about the potential global repercussions.

Frumpf was crouched on a stool in a large room that housed a hundred computer monitors, each with a technician making keystrokes.

"I don't want any of you to eat, piss, or sleep until we trace the origin of this rumor. I want to know the first place this appeared on the web," Frumpf demanded.

Frumpf barged out of the room with a bit of a limp he had developed from having to walk a certain way as not to dislodge his prosthetic dick. He made his way back to the oval office where Snopes was waiting along with Frumpf's chief of staff.

"I hope you didn't have anything to do with this leak mister. This was a classified situation. What do you have for me? It better be good," Frumpf insisted.

Snopes had no choice but to give Frumpf the only good news he could think of. He told the president he could reverse the problem if he stopped being evil. Frumpf looked at Snopes with the eyes of a demon and claimed he didn't have an evil bone in his body. He asked Snopes how he came by this preposterous theory in the first place. Snopes said he has been researching *vanishing penis syndrome* and he believes this could be the solution. Frumpf spit back that even if he was a prick about certain things, it didn't mean he was evil.

"By who's fucking standard would this so-called *syndrome* redemption be evaluated?" Frumpf asked.

Snopes said it was all about public perception, and therefore by endorsing equal rights, constitutional freedoms, environmental concerns, etc., society was likely to see him in a favorable light. Frumpf argued that there was no way to make everyone happy, insisting the country was philosophically almost divided in half, touting that the larger half supported him. Snopes didn't point out that Frumpf lost the popular vote. Frumpf continued, claiming that there was never consensus when it comes to public perception. With a touch of humanitarian brilliance, Snopes said,

"Then bridge the gap, sir. It will make you the greatest leader that ever lived, which sounds penile regenerating to me."

The president paced the room, occasionally doing a little hip thrust to center his awkward faux privates. Under his breath, he kept murmuring,

"The greatest leader that ever lived. Bridge the gap..."

*33

When word about Frumpf's missing penis was the talk in a sleepy town like Woodstock, I realized it wouldn't be long before I was dragged away in shackles, and thrown into a gulag. There were too many clues leading to me, meaning the intelligence community was bound to put my face to the blame. To temporarily relieve my stress, I imagined what would happen if they accused George Clooney. When Lana returned from the farmer's market, I told her I had an epiphany the two of us should spend the next couple of years visiting the world's most renowned spiritual sights. I told her we could visit the Uluru Plateau in Australia coveted by the aborigines for its six-hundred-million-year-old energy field. We could visit Easter Island in the Polynesian triangle, and experience the ancient statuary. Picnic at Stonehenge listening for the lessons told through the ether of the prehistoric dead that were sacredly buried there. Lana hung on every word and responded by saying she felt like she went on the journey just listening to my description, but two years? I tried to illustrate the importance of being spontaneous in life. I insisted travel was the key to global understanding and world peace. I told her that we could learn the ancient techniques of the Chinese herbalists in Lijiang province, and bring the healing methods back to this haven. She looked at me with the utmost fascination but said,

"Very sweet Sheldon, maybe we could take off for a couple of weeks next year."

How could I tell her there might not be a next year? There was no way I could let her know it was me who dedicked Richard Frumpf in an effort to save the world. It didn't coincide with her non-judgmental, aromatherapized existence. After hearing myself describe the fantasy itinerary, I realized it was time for me alone to go on such a journey, and I would have to say goodbye to this tantric tryst.

Snopes had been calling me for days, but I was done with the cloak and dagger shit. I did my deed for humanity. It was now time to run. On my way to the bus station, I was amazed to see Snopes coming out of a store. I was about to duck away, but he spotted me so I decided I might as well see what he is up to now. First I wanted to know if he had my cell phone triangulated to find my location. He was honest and claimed at our last meeting I told him an old friend made me some Mu tea. He investigated my former girlfriends, and when Lana the yoga teacher from Woodstock came up he had a strong hunch that is where the tea came from. I commended him on his sleuthing abilities and informed him I was preparing to flee the country for good. He claimed the reason he was looking for me was that he had gathered a bunch of theories that we could try to attempt to get Frumpf his dick back. I reminded him I had no interest in curing Frumpf unless he could somehow change for the good, which we both deemed unlikely over and over again. Snopes shared how he'd explained to Frumpf there was a possibility that a reversal of evil might bring back his cock. He said the president wasn't even able to accept he was a prick. Snopes suggested to me we figure out a cure, make a long list of humane concerns and barter with Frumpf. I said I didn't have any new magic spells to go to and the whole thing was way too complicated. Snopes said I should suit myself, but he hoped I didn't mind looking over my shoulder around the clock because they will eventually come looking for me. Out of the corner of my eye, I noticed a suspicious looking guy talking into a phone with purpose as he observed Snopes and me. Maybe they were having Snopes followed at this point, or maybe paranoia was setting in, either way, it was time to go so I wished Snopes luck, assuring him if I have any epiphanies he would be the first to know. Then I asked him for one last favor. We got into his car and drove off. I took my baseball cap and fit it onto my headrest so it would appear someone was sitting there as Snopes suggested. When we turned the corner, I jumped out of the car and hid behind a tree as he kept driving. While I watched, another car came along following Snopes from a distance. It was the same suspicious fellow I saw checking us out.

*34

The parish of Amesbury, England, was established approximately 8000 B.C. and is the oldest continuously occupied settlement in the United Kingdom. The Amesbury Travel Lodge was a basic, no frills, clean hotel, and just a short ride to a popular bunch of rocks commonly known as Stonehenge. It wasn't the spiritual mumbo jumbo I concocted to entice Lana that brought me here. As long as I am going to be on the lam, I decided to try and understand the nature of my vanishing penis power. A world famous pile of twenty-five ton, stone phallic monoliths was a good place to begin. In retrospect, I may have made a mistake and might have been better served to start my journey in someplace warmer and exotic. When the feds come looking for me, I would hate for my last bit of freedom to have been spent in this cold, gloomy town.

The prehistoric monument itself was formidable, yet at the same time inviting due to its iconic familiarity. It was way more impressive in person than other landmarks I have seen up close, like the Eifel Tower, which was more spectacular at night and illuminated from afar. The geographic configuration of the stones was begging to be a complete circle but fell short, appearing like a Lego-set for giants that had been abandoned in a hurry. I sat as close to the center as I could calculate, and faced the side that was most cylindrical in its conformity. The air was permeated with a light mist that not only humidified my skin and hair but also imbued my consciousness with molecules of the mystic. I found myself engaging in a breathing technique my mother had taught me. Clearing my mind while cognizant of my recent escapades was not an easy task. After a few moments, I felt a sudden surge of energy and opened my eyes to what appeared to be the 13-foot monoliths fading away before me. I suddenly felt empowered to reverse their disappearance. As my mind isolated its focus on their vanishing form, their physical presence seemed to be instantly revitalized. My attention was immediately averted to the sky where a puffy group of clouds swirled counter-clockwise with an unnatural velocity. A cold rain drenched me back to reality, making me aware it was time to seek shelter.

*35

A fat computer technician stood in front of Frumpf's desk at the oval office while the president looked over his report. Turned out the first mention of Frumpf's missing penis was made by Larry Silverberg, who happened to be Florence Cohen's brother-in-law. Yes, the game of "I promise not tell" has many levels and in this case it didn't take long to make it to the top. When Frumpf was made aware that the wife of Valina's therapist was related to the rumormonger, his rage was soaked with vengeance. When Frumpf presented Valina with the allegations, she swore up and down she trusted Idsel, and that it was impossible he would share what they discussed in therapy. Frumpf first wanted to know if she had mentioned his missing penis with the doc, to which she claimed she couldn't recall. His attitude with his daughter was softer than with most, so he commended her for answering like a true politician, but vehemently relayed she needed to remember. Valina told him what she talks about in therapy was her business, to which he replied,

"Not when it is a matter of national security."

Valina roared back that his missing penis had nothing to do with security, and everything to do with his insecurity. She made him promise he would not do anything to compromise her relationship with Idsel who she described as the singular soul that keeps her sane. Frumpf promised, but his sincerity was worth its weight in tin.

*36

The Wednesday Bloga exercise was a series of planks that Thelma did in front of a mirror to be sure her back was straight. When she answered the door in her workout attire, she was not expecting to see Snopes again. Without even a hello she blurted out that she had no idea where I was hiding. Snopes said that wasn't his reason for being there, and requested a chat. Thelma's automatic hosting reflex kicked right in. Snopes filled her in on the penis caper developments and claimed he had it from solid sources they were about to interrogate him in a more serious manner, and are closing in on me. He then dropped the serious demeanor and admitted his visit was to see if it was possible to obtain more of Thelma's gefilte fish. Snopes shared he was never one to partake in drugs of any kind, that he has had to be careful with alcohol, but what he experienced the other day was magnificent. Thelma attempted to play dumb, but Snopes said he tasted something in her dish that was not there for flavor. He noted the timing of how long it supposedly takes to get off on an edible coincided with her "hors d'oeuvres." He assured her that although he was not interested in seeing her arrested, drugging a federal agent is a serious charge, and all she had to do to mitigate the crime was repeat the offense. He shared the experience he had with his plants and said for the first time in his life he felt happy for no reason. It was as if someone had cast a magic spell on him. Snopes left with a large jar of gefilte fish. Thelma briefed him on the recommended dosage and thanked him for being a good sport about the situation.

When Valina arrived at Idsel's office, he was in session. She anxiously paced around the waiting room until she couldn't wait a second longer, and then barged in on him. Fortunately, his current patient, a familiar looking black sports star, was leaving. The patient recognized Valina from the news, and shook his head in disapproval, asking her if there was no line of decency her family wouldn't cross. He grabbed his hat off of the rack, and then exited. Valina took a moment to let his discredit sink in. She then turned towards Idsel and asked point blank if he had told anyone about the missing penis admission. The deep look in his eyes said volumes. He pondered his future as a therapist as he had broken the mighty moral code, and had betrayed a patient, which put him in the middle of a major scandal. He sat down on the couch, and said,

"I told my wife."

Valina, less vindictive than her dad, seemed to understand. She sat beside him in a consoling manner, softly explaining Frumpf was on the warpath after tracing a blog to Idsel's brother-in-law. She claimed she made him promise not to retaliate, but they both knew her dad was full of shit. Idsel shared he had been told so many secrets in his day, but this one was the whopper that got away. He claimed he needed to share it, emphasizing that for every ounce of trust Valina had in him there was no multiplier that could increase the amount of faith he had in his wife's confidence. He apologized for her and said,

"Apparently, a president's missing penis is a secret way too extraordinary to withhold."

Valina started to freak out and insisted she didn't want their doctor/patient relationship to end. And then out of nowhere she yelled out,

"He did it! He did it to me!" Then broke down in tears.

Had Snopes been warned that today was the day the feds would abduct him to Washington he would not have ingested a healthy portion of Thelma's fish. Although he was theoretically a fed himself, they were not forthcoming regarding the nature of his detainment. He was well aware it had to do with Frumpf's 'predickament,' as he liked to call it while enhancing the accent on the word dick.

The four-hour drive to D.C. in the back of a cushy SUV was momentous in his current state. The scenery along the way took on a fascinating quality. Something as mundane as a man walking his dog appeared magnificent. Snopes would occasionally break the silence with a banal inquiry, but other than an occasional wisecrack from the driver the agents were tightlipped. When they arrived at the White House, the gate security guard requested Snopes' identification. He told the agents they should have given him more time to get ready because his wallet is back in New York. After a bunch of procedural falderal, he was permitted entry and taken straight to a holding room. In his stoned state, Snopes thought to himself, with Frumpf's current situation the last place he should be seen is a *holding room*.

Sitting alone in a room across from the president seemed absurd. Snopes wished that Frumpf had also eaten some of Thelma's fish to level the playing field, as the apparent intensity of Frumpf's face warned that a dire confrontation was imminent. There was no more time to figure out a cure, Frumpf bellowed. He confirmed that Snopes was a prime suspect now, and unless he gives him something tangible it's game over. Unsure what that even meant, Snopes decided to shared the truth. Like me, he left Thelma and Norman out of the loop and said I was at the rally in Kentucky for the opportunity to make the president's penis disappear. The president claimed I was the one who saved his life, so didn't understand why I would do that. He also didn't understand what a vanishing penis has to do with anything. Snopes filled him in on my confessed inability to sit idly by while any human being was assassinated, even Frumpf. He added that I truly believed the subsequent scenario was universal intervention to allow the opportunity to vanish his dick.

"They didn't want to see you dead sir, they only wanted to soften your attitude. Kind of like fixing a dog," Snopes added.

Frumpf immediately jumped on the "they" part of the statement, which Snopes tried to shrug off by saying he just meant me. Frumpf interjected, claiming Thelma was obviously in on it. For the first time in his interaction with the president, Snopes was impressed; Frumpf remembered Thelma's name. Then he speculated Frumpf remembered because Thelma must have looked hot in her evening gown that night. The president questioned why Snopes hadn't shared all these facts sooner. Snopes claimed he was trying to confirm the details because of the seriousness of the allegations. When the president asked where I was now, Snopes said he had met with me in Woodstock a couple of days ago but hasn't seen or heard from me since. Then with the intensity of Zeus, Frumpf asked,

"Does he have the fucking ability to make it come back?"

With the most brilliance a stoned man could muster, Snopes said I was out seeking that very solution, an answer that may have induced Frumpf to give me more time before tracking me down.

*39

The Grotto of Massabielle is in the southwestern French town of Lourdes. Every year millions of people flock to the manicured springs whose waters are reported to perform miracles through the biblically based healing properties. At the moment all I needed healing from was another night sleeping on a dreaded overstuffed hotel pillow. The anxiety of being aware my days as a free man were numbered became less burdensome than I predicted. It occurred to me that eventually, the Frumpf administration might hold something over me that will require solid negotiation, and though it is the last thing I hope to do, I would at least like the option of being able to restore his privates. My recent revitalization vision at Stonehenge gave me hope my journey of discovery may lead to the ability to reverse the effects of my power. One problem was, I have no way of confirming it without actually performing the task.

My issue with this Catholic Church divine destination was the same problem I have with all of their consecrated theme parks dotted throughout their almost 200 million acres worldwide, *the story*. In this case, a fourteen-year-old peasant strolling around the grounds of a local garbage dump bumps into immaculate Mary, and is given a to-do list; build a chapel, invite the sick, and invest in the 100 acres around it. To be fair, I have no ability to discern whose magic makes the most sense, especially because on the surface my crystal lewd persuasion makes the least. When I got in line to approach the miraculous spring, I realized another big reason why this particular pilgrimage port was a mistake. Who wants to hang around people that travel great distances to heal? What are they healing from? Is it transmittable? Am I standing next to a deadly virus victim that was too afraid to declare his malady, and instead decided to put the matter into the hands of God?

As an aside, I wondered if after God had cured infectious diseases he used hand sanitizer.

40

For a guy who spends most of his adult life in an office, Idsel was not excited about being summoned to Frumpf's oval version. He was aware it was unlikely to be a pleasant visit. Frumpf's pastime of practicing irrational conduct made Idsel expect the worst. Upon entering the west wing presidential domain, Idsel was greeted with more courtesy than imagined. Frumpf motioned for him to sit on the couch, and asked what kind of beverage the good doctor would like. The president even joked that if they didn't have his preference, he would send the vice president out to get it. Being a seasoned psychologist who understands human behavior made Idsel more troubled about Frumpf's demeanor than had he appeared to be angry. Idsel knew ensuing manipulation when he saw it and said a glass of water would be fine. Frumpf recommended he have a little scotch with that order to help with the discussion they were about to have. Idsel knew it was not the time to negotiate, so he relented. As they sipped their cocktails, Frumpf went on to give Idsel a little history of his childhood revealing how his father made him feel like he was never good enough. He went on to almost apologize for the way he may have overcompensated in bringing up Valina to the point of smothering. Idsel was a pro at just listening, which is what he did as the president continued. Frumpf claimed he knows Idsel violated Valina's confidentiality, and although it was only to his wife, it was still wrong. Idsel acknowledged by nodding his head. Frumpf said because he is an understanding man who appreciates Valina's respect for Idsel, he was willing to come to an agreement. Whatever treaty the president was about to offer, Idsel knew it was going to be a devil on the dotted line transaction. Frumpf then said,

"Plain and simple, all I want to know is everything my daughter has said about me in therapy."

*41

When Thelma answered her cell phone at the beauty parlor, the other ladies noticed her concern. Snopes called to inform her it was likely the feds were heading to her home to apprehend her for her role in the president's dick disappearance. He told her Norman was out of harm's way for now, but she might want to vanish with him for a while until the heat died down. When she hung up she concealed her panic by telling Dorothy, the hairdresser, she decided to go platinum blonde. She also called Norman insisting he meet her at their favorite getaway cabin to have an important discussion.

Snopes was set free based on Frumpf's belief he was the president's best chance of locating me to help get his penis back. The media buzz was now out of hand. Even Fox news, Frumpf's right arm of propaganda could not ignore reporting about his missing appendage and was avidly working on how to blame it on Iran. Between the pressures of running a country while unqualified, and losing his primary motivation in life, Frumpf was on the verge of suicide. Idsel deftly rerouted Frumpf's request to infiltrate his daughter's therapy sessions by suggesting Frumpf allow Idsel to counsel the president through this debacle, and maybe even find a way to restore his penis through psychological means. Even the seasoned conman was no match for the insightful, clever mind manipulations of this renowned therapist. What Idsel realized was that no one understood the mechanisms that vanished Frumpf's cock, so anything he proposed was possible. There was nothing he could suggest that was more absurd than the initial event itself.

*42

When Thelma arrived at the cabin, Norman was pacing the porch in a state of worry. All Thelma said on the phone was she wanted to have a "discussion," which could mean anything, but had the same undertone as "we need to talk." At first, he didn't recognize his wife, who appeared younger and sexier in her new platinum hairdo. After a hug and some chitchat, Thelma shared the latest details Snopes had provided. Norman doubted he could endure being a fugitive, and shared that even the 'Handy Randy' episode gave him heartburn. Thelma sang Canada's praises and pointed out her cousin Rhoda would treat them like visiting royalty. Norman had so many questions; the house, his job, the bills, his car... As he went on and on Thelma boiled it down to two choices; incarceration for a unique version of treason, or Canada. Thelma had already struck a deal with Snopes exchanging the gefilte fish recipe for help getting across the border. When Norman realized they were not only leaving their whole world behind but would have to sneak across the Canadian border, he tried to talk her into hiding out in his brother Murray's basement in Philadelphia. After a night of intermittent sleep at the cabin, Norman awoke to find Thelma gone. She had left a note affirming that hiding out at his brother's was a fine idea, and promised she would reunite with him when the dust settled. Even though he knew where she was heading, the note said it would be safer for all if he didn't know where she was going. Norman carefully folded the note and put it in his shirt pocket as if he was tucking Thelma there herself.

*43

Millions upon millions are spent every year attempting to predict societal trends. Experts weigh in regarding the economy, politics, and entertainment, all aimed at wrapping their legs around the future so corporate commerce can bang their buck into oblivion. Of course, millions are also spent influencing these trends so companies can inject need into the spongy mind of the masses, so they concur, conform, and consume. Still, all that money and all those geniuses would never have anticipated Frumpf's subsequent phenomenon. Initially, the backlash was brutal, as everyone exhumed hearsay for confirmation of his dicklessness to use as yet another reason to end his right to govern. But the repercussions experienced an odd counteract. Women's groups protested the theme that being without a penis made you unworthy. The transgender community was thrilled with the prospect that one could rid oneself of an unwanted appendage sans surgery. Even certain Liberal factions pushed the premise that maybe now Frumpf would think with his heart instead. It was brought to his attention by his staff that the approval rating they had failed to enhance was now rocketing towards the heavens due to some kind of neuter accord. The media began to embrace the public's attitude that his castration made him more human. All the major magazines were vying for the exclusive cover photo of what was now being called the *Executive Zone*. It was hard to believe, but having nothing between your legs was now seen as sexy. Producers were making zone porn, even gay zone porn where men would simulate giving head to an empty space. In his cockless condition, Frumpf was now becoming people's *Unsexiest* man alive.

When I came across this shocking sensation online, I felt perplexed. Had my crotch magic made things worse for the world? I saw on Facebook that Caitlin Jenner was offering a million dollars to anyone that could connect her to the person that dedicked Frumpf. Although Frumpf was the celebrated freak of the moment, I was now the coveted mystery magician who could turn your dreams of dicklessness into reality with a simple stare. I was stunned that the public was familiar with the process, and wondered if it had been leaked by the president himself. Was this brand of notoriety better or worse than being hunted by the Feds? Imagine you are found out to be the one that could cure cancer; you would be hunted down by everyone who was inflicted. Of course making a dick disappear was not as popular as disease ratification, but I was still perceived as a miracle worker. I was not the healing spring at Lourdes; I was genitalia Jesus himself. I broke away from the computer because my mind began to spin out about all the potential implications and contraindications of my unwanted power. Also, reading about the sexual ramifications made me think of Thelma, and wish she were here.

As they approached customs in Snopes' borrowed car, Thelma questioned again how confident he was regarding his friend's passport working to gain her entry into Canada. He insisted she relax and repeated she should only speak if she is questioned. They rehearsed the whole scenario many times during the seven-hour drive, and though Snopes was aware of Thelma's gift of spontaneous gab, he made her promise not to improvise. It was late afternoon, so the line to pass through was not busy. As they pulled up to the border control, they were asked for their passports. Snopes handed the guy both. The guard spent an elongated moment comparing Anna Denton's passport photo to Thelma, and then asked,

"What sign are you?"

Snopes had Thelma memorize Anna's birthday, but didn't delve into astrology, and Thelma had no idea about the corresponding sign of the Zodiac.

"Astrology is the devil's work. The only star I follow is the one in Bethlehem," she stated.

The guard looked at Snopes who just shrugged. He seemed satisfied and handed back the passports welcoming them to Canada. In forty-five minutes they arrived at cousin Rhoda's place; a lovely country house on an acre of land. Rhoda couldn't have been more accommodating, and being a widow, she was delighted to make Snopes' acquaintance.

Rhoda was astounded to hear about Thelma's Frumpf fiasco and impressed she had the "gumption" to pull it off. While Rhoda prepared a tantalizing salmon dinner, Thelma completely captivated her with her description of the White House gala, which included the night in the Lincoln Bedroom. Since Rhoda thought Thelma was happily married, she omitted the adulterous sexcapades for now. The next morning at breakfast while Thelma wished Snopes a safe trip back, Rhoda chimed in that "Snopesy" has decided to extend his stay. Thelma eyed the two of them, safely assuming that the other guestroom had not been used last night. As Turns out, Rhoda and Snopes had a great deal in common, she being a botanist with an ability to cook a mean barbecued chicken. Rhoda was entranced by Snopes' FBI background and revealed she'd always wanted her very own Elliot Ness.

*45

The quest to perfect my surgical sorcery wore off, and now all I wanted to do was rid myself of all power and popularity. In life, I have mostly been a recluse. It's hard for me to trust people, as it appears most are mining for validation, minerals I believe we should excavate in ourselves. Had I wound up famous for pasteurizing the toxic tyrant I may have welcomed the moniker, but transforming Frumpf into a sex god propels my id into an ostrich hole. I have somehow managed to elevate Hitler's approval rating. What I wish I had done is use the power to give him a vagina instead so he could go fuck himself.

What was also pushing on my psyche was the realization that I was homeless. I was now a nomad, circumstantially banished from my homeland. And to top things off, I was missing Thelma. How screwed up is that? I castrated someone for being evil, and now I'm fixated on Norman's wife. Maybe it's the forbidden sex, the excitement of irresponsible romance, or the biggest sin of all, I might actually be falling in love with her.

The media pressure to present the Executive Zone to the public was increasing. Citizens of the conspiratorial ilk were beginning to speculate that the whole thing was a ploy *trumped up* by Frumpf to bolster his approval. At this point they wanted to see his empty crotch as much as his tax returns. They speculated that maybe the missing penis plot was a desperate fabrication designed to distract from a Russian oil deal in the arctic worth a half trillion dollars. When Frumpf insisted to his advisors they furnish Fox News with an exclusive crotch preview, they argued that the public would charge collusion, and make allegations that the images were Photoshopped. Instead they insisted it should appear on the cover of Time magazine.

The Time magazine photographer was full of trepidation as he entered the heavily guarded, windowless studio. He had won awards for capturing military maneuvers in Iraq, war torn villages in Sarajevo, and the horrors of hurricane Katrina, but the idea that he was about to photograph what wasn't there fucked with his normal artistic sensibility. Frumpf displayed a lack of cordiality as he hoped they would send a female photographer so he could experience the effect his Executive Zone had on the opposite sex. The lensman ignored his dissatisfaction, and instead discussed the tone of the shot itself. How does one tastefully shoot the president's naked crotch? There was nothing in history to compare it to. It was almost like photographing Monica giving Clinton a faux-blow. Should Frumpf be wearing a suit from the waste up? Should it be his *Zone* without depicting the president himself? Unable to get a handle on the style, the photographer asked if it would be possible to see the *Zone* to help make a determination. Frumpf cleared the room of everyone else. Once they were alone, Frumpf joked this is the first, and hopefully last time he would ever drop his drawers for a man. As the photographer observed Frumpf's blank crotch, the president explained they didn't have a large window of time because he had them remove the catheter temporarily as to not make his Zone look dire. He would soon need it reattached to take a leak. The cameraman immediately began clicking away.

When the Time issue came out depicting Frumpf dressed in a suit with his pants lowered just below his crotch, and shrugging off his missing dick with a smirk, it sold more copies than any issue of any magazine in history. Princess

Diana's death, the World Trade Center, nothing came close to the five million copies that flew off the stands the first day. Now with an image to validate the story the world went wild. Halloween costumes were fabricated that made one's crotch mimic the Zone. Viagra's new ad campaign claimed it worked on every man but one. Trojan condoms promoted that using their product was 'almost' the safest sex in the world. A guy who was already the most famous man on the globe due to his unlikely rise to power was now beyond fame, an awkward icon, a perpetual joke, and a new concept of human being all rolled up into one. There was someone though, who was not happy about his penile publicity. Teresa Frumpf was irate; when she barged into the oval office with the magazine in hand she could not be consoled.

"How could you embarrass us like this? Why didn't you talk it over with me first? It is disgraceful, I want a divorce, today," she yelled, then continued her tirade, "What kind of man shows off his, his nothing? Do you think this is all some kind of big joke? You have a daughter. I hope you are happy because even if some magic man brings back your cock I wouldn't touch it if it were the last one there is. You will be hearing from my lawyer."

Teresa stormed out of the oval office as Valina was entering. She didn't even stop to greet her stepdaughter. Frumpf asked Valina if she was there to berate him as well. Valina claimed she wanted to thank Frumpf for not punishing Idsel. She then told him she understands these are crazy times that must be very confusing and unsettling, and that she is going to take some time off to process some stuff. Frumpf asked,

"Time off from what? Process what kind of stuff?"

Valina dropped a bombshell that would have been nuclear even without Teresa's recent demand for a divorce.

"I believe you molested me, father. I need to see if there is a way to forgive you and move on."

The look on Frumpf's face began to rebel, but she added,

"Please don't say anything or deny it because you will only make it worse. I do love you daddy, but I am not sure where our relationship will go from here."

She exited the office leaving him doubly dumfounded. Even dickless he felt castrated again.

47

Two FBI agents visited Thelma and Norman's place, but no one was there. Without hesitating, they broke in and began to search for clues to their whereabouts. Norman had not been to work, and Thelma was completely MIA. The agents noticed the fruit on the table was extremely overripe and the mailbox overloaded. It was obvious no one had been there for days. After some time, one of the agents opened up the fridge and poured a glass of orange juice. The other agent asked if there was anything worth eating. He spotted a large container of gefilte fish and set it on the counter. To someone that is not familiar with gefilte fish, it is mostly made up of whitefish and matzah meal and resembles light colored shit floating in a jar. The agent knew what it was because his grandmother used to make it, so they decided to give it a try. They found it tasty and consumed it all.

A few days of excessive brotherly lecturing was enough to make Norman chance going home. He had already missed a few of days of work, and things were busy right now at Flimsy Fork, so he was needed. He figured if the feds were actively looking they would eventually find him, so he may as well sleep in his own bed. He was surprised to see a strange vehicle in the driveway, and the front door of his house wide open. He contemplated the possibilities and hoped Thelma had returned. Nothing Norman considered would have prepared him for what he was about to witness. The two agents sat on the living room couch, poking fun at Norman and Thelma's old wedding video. When they saw Norman enter, they feebly attempted to exhibit professional decorum. Norman saw the empty jar of gefilte fish on the kitchen table, providing him with the gist of the unlikely scenario. Instead of confronting them in what he assumed to be a highly altered state, he sat with the agents and described some back-stories about the people in the videos. For the next hour the three of them laughed through selected parts of Norman's family video collection, but when the show was over their new kinship didn't prevent them from insisting that they still needed to detain Thelma. When he claimed her whereabouts was a mystery, they said they respected his protective nature but didn't believe him. Norman showed them the note in his pocket Thelma left him, confirming his story. The two agents inspected it, held it up to the lamp, and claimed it looked valid. As if all official business was complete, they asked if he had any strong coffee.

*48

After Frumpf's confrontation with both his wife and his daughter, he immediately summoned Idsel to his office. He insisted the therapist tell him everything Valina shared regarding what he called "her allegations" regarding the molestation. Idsel said that before they delve into her private sessions, which he had no plans of doing, they should first review Frumpf's memory of such events.

As if he was on the witness stand the president stated,

"Did I have an overly stimulated crush on my daughter? Yes. Did I get aroused quite a few times when she sat on my lap? Yes. Did I fantasize about having sex with her while masturbating? I have. Did I ever purposely fondle or display inappropriate behavior? Absolutely not. Aren't those things normal Doc? Don't all family members experience lewd thoughts they would never act upon?"

Idsel thought about Frumpf's question and answered,

"Many people have a variety of sexual thoughts that could be deemed inappropriate, but there is a long road between thoughts and action. A doctor surely has sexual fantasies about their patients, and visa versa, especially because they have forged a deep trusting relationship. Do you think it's fine if I harbored a fantasy about having sex with Valina?"

Frumpf's eyebrows almost rose off his head. He wasn't sure how to respond, and unlike the way he deals with governmental issues he spent a few minutes thinking about this.

"Do you have sexual fantasies about my daughter," Frumpf asked.

Idsel said he never shares personal thoughts like that with a patient and was attempting to illustrate to Frumpf the emotion attached to it all. Frumpf repeated his request to know what Valina had told him. Idsel asked Frumpf if he could identify the emotion attached to his need to know. The president said he had some major separation anxiety. Idsel asked if it was the same type of anxiety he imagined families must be going through when they are torn apart due to his unconstitutional immigration policies. Or intense as the emotion a spouse or parent must experience when a loved one is shot down by the police just for being black. Frumpf ignored the fact that Idsel's response was out of the realm of conventional therapy and said,

"You gave me a great idea."

Suddenly an aid rushed into the office claiming there was a 'situation' Frumpf needed to attend to.

*49

The valley of 1000 Lingas is a Cambodian architectural site along the Stung Kbal Spean River where an endless variety of phallic carvings grace the stone riverbed along with various Hindu mythological entities. I know of it through photos I have seen of my late mother's trip to Angkor Wat during her youth. A spiritual site laced with rock penises seemed thematically potent regarding my current dilemma. Maybe I could glean some more insight about the power I am so awkwardly wielding. Angkor Wat is a major tourist destination. The area boasts a complex of stone temples whose walls were intricately carved depicting ancient tales and was known as the largest religious monument in the world. I checked into a hotel called the Red Piano and spent the night checking out the city of Siem Reap and its cultural distractions. The following morning I arranged for a guide to take me to what I now thought of as Penis River. The jeep ride into the jungle was bumpy, and the road was not always easy to follow. There were blotches of red paint on some of the trees, warnings not to veer off in those directions, as it was possible there were still land mines left over from the horrid Pol Pot regime. Quite a few local Cambodians are missing limbs due to an unfortunate misstep, not to mention many a cow that were instantly turned to steak and burger. When we arrived at the site, no one else was around. My first perception was that it was just a simple stream surrounded by large turquoise butterflies. Closer inspection revealed the phallic carvings along the bank. My guide told me that when the river flowed above these sacred cock carvings, the water becomes holy, and supposedly stimulates fertility. He led me to the grand finale; a small waterfall one sits under to be cleansed with the sacred splash.

As I pondered the lagoon where the waterfall fell, I sensed something. To label it a cosmic calling may be overkill, but I was being drawn into the pool. I disrobed down to my boxer-briefs, and slowly waded my way in. The water temperature was warmer than I expected, and the way the morning sun filtered through the falls gave it an odd orange glow. The pool was only waist deep. When I reached its center, I sat in the very spot where thousands of Hindu priests and devotees had once reverently perched, allowing the holy water to also have its way with me. After only a minute the atmosphere began to transmute. The butterfly population multiplied as the sun moved higher in the sky heating the water flow to a temperature that felt custom made for my body. I suddenly found myself shifting my position so instead of facing outward I was now looking directly into the grotto. The sunlight became the lamp of nature's projector, and through the filter of the falls cast an image on the grotto wall. At first, it was unclear, but as I continued to stare, it materialized into the image of President Richard J. Frumpf. Suddenly, the sun moved behind a cloud and the water turned cold. I stood up, and walked to the bank of the lagoon reuniting with the guide who was waiting patiently, wearing a smile that hinted he knew I had experienced something profound.

*50

The Situation Room at the White House was no one's favorite place to be. Apparently, Bashar al-Assad, the current president of Syria had used Sarin gas on his citizens, killing a large number of children. The use of chemical weapons was deemed illegal and inhumane by the international community, as if any weaponry in battle could be considered humane. This act of war required a US response, and it was frighteningly up to Frumpf to make the call. After listening to all the opinions and advice of his military intelligence, he responded in an Idsel-esque tone by asking everyone in the room how they would feel if their child was the victim of this lethal gas that causes instantaneous suffocation due to lung muscle paralysis. He added that although a response is warranted, violent retaliation is not always the answer, and suggested they bring Assad in for a chat. His advisors told him that even if Assad agreed, inviting him to the White House at this time might be perceived as supporting his actions. Much to his administration's dismay, Frumpf insisted on holding a press conference to address the situation. His staff members were having fits of panic and tried to convince him to at least speak from a script prepared by one of his speechwriters. Frumpf claimed to be on top of the situation and said he didn't need fluff to pull this one off.

51

Stone temple after stone temple was my plan for the day as I tried to imagine what these places were like when they were fully accessorized and operational. Most of the furnishings, art, and relics had been stolen by the military over the years. The meager items that were preserved were housed in a museum hours away in Phnom Penh. As the dollar-docents tagged along trying to enrich their pockets and my experience at the same time, I was made privy to the tales of hierarchy carved into the walls. It was possible to ascertain the level of a figure's nobility based on the number of umbrellas that were held above their head. I would have paid way more than a dollar if the docent could explain the significance of seeing Frumpf's image on the grotto wall. Was it my mind playing tricks on me? Did I imagine it because the dickless dictator was in my thoughts around the clock? Or was it possible there was a spiritual implication I was supposed to process that would give me greater insight into my power? There was one thing I felt certain about, that I was done searching, and ready to figure out a plan to deal with the chaos I had created. It was too bad Lana did not accompany me to this place because I was sure it would be the highlight of her existence. But it was still the thoughts of Thelma that were calling out to me. It wasn't even the sexual ambitions at this point. I felt a need to bounce all of my recent mystical revelations off of her to try and make sense of it all. She must have read my mind because when I checked my email, there was a message from her:

HI SHELDON. SORRY ABOUT ALL CAPS BUT MY HOST'S COMPUTER KEYBOARD HAS BEEN COMPROMISED DUE TO A ROGUE CUP OF COFFEE. GOOD THING IT WASN'T YOU KNOW WHOS WHITE CARPET. I HOPE YOU ARE DOING WELL. IT SEEMS LIKE YESTERDAY WE WERE TOGETHER ON LAKE ONTARIO AND I WISH WE WERE BOTH BACK THERE AGAIN. CHINA IS FABULOUS, WHY DON'T YOU MEET ME AT THE PALACE ON FRIDAY. MISS YOU. THELMA

I read the note a few times, and it made absolutely no sense. First of all we have never been to Lake Ontario together, and Thelma once told me China was not one of her bucket list destinations. The palace? I printed out the message at the Internet café, and then took a walk through the large

Cambodian market where the colorful textiles and artifacts were fascinating and inspiring.

YESTERDAY WE WERE IN LAKE ONTARIO...Hmm maybe she is in Toronto I thought. WISH WE WERE BOTH THERE AGAIN...She wants me to come there...CHINA...PALACE? I returned to the café and Googled restaurants in Toronto. It wasn't that shocking to see there was a Chinese restaurant called "The Mandarin Palace" right near Lake Ontario. Now that I felt I had possibly deciphered her semi-cryptic letter, I also realized that anyone who has seen a Sherlock Holmes film could have decoded it in seconds.

52

High anxiety befell Frumpf's political handlers. In the White House Rose Garden stood a lone podium set up in front of the largest audience of press representatives invited since the beginning of Frumpf's reign. The Republican majority leader approached Frumpf in the hall, telling him that whatever he says today could have a lasting effect on the future of the Republican Party and implored Frumpf to reconsider running his speech by him before he faced the media. Frumpf shushed him, and swore what he was about to say would ensure the party's hold on the Senate for generations to come, and that no one gives a better speech than him. When Frumpf approached the podium, the cameras began to click at a rapid pace. He waved hello to a few of the reporters, smiled at others, and then began to speak,

"My fellow Americans. As you are all overly aware, I have been dealt with what many would consider a major handicap recently. Especially you Brandon."

He was referring to Brandon Klink of the Washington Times who had a reputation of being quite the ladies man. The knowing press corps laughed at the comment.

Frumpf continued,

"As I am sure as with anyone who faces new obstacles in life, we learn to adapt, to adjust to the changes God delivers. If these changes are in fact divine intervention, the results must be beneficial to humanity. This may come as a shock to you all, but there have been times in my life where I have been arrogant and disrespectful towards women."

There is a smattering of laughter, but for the most part the reporters are amazed to hear Frumpf admit to any personal shortcomings.

He continued,

"My recent change in anatomy has shifted more of my thoughts to, not just my upper brain, but also my heart. It is suddenly clear we can no longer hope for human sustainability without replacing ideological dogma with a blanket of compassion. I am sure you are all aware of the recent act of rationalized terror imposed on the people of Syria by their leader, Assad. There are those in the war room right now that think the globe is a video game where slaughtering foreigners is not murder, but merely a concept called collateral damage. They are half right because it is definitely damage. These kinds of activities damage our hearts, our future, and the health of our environment, which is said by scientists to be going through a broken heart of its own right now. So it is within the spirit of peace and human prosperity I am inviting Assad, as well as any other world leader who cares to participate in a summit to strategize a better plan towards global unity. Thank you for your attention, God bless the United States of America, and God bless us all."

As what just transpired sank in, every member of the audience rose in applause. Frumpf's cohorts standing in the wings looked at each other perplexed as to whether he just hit a home run, or committed political suicide. That night, the evening news anchors all acted like Frumpf had suddenly become presidential. No one seemed to notice or point out that most of what he said was guilefully plagiarized.

53

Airport cab drivers sometimes act like they're members of the taxi elite. Sir Hitesh Kapoor dropped me off in front of the King George Hotel right near the lake. Instead of checking in I immediately wandered off in search of the Mandarin Palace. Although I wasn't positive Thelma would be there, the anticipation had traveled to my loins. Feeling like the Daniel Craig of castration, I walked cautiously through the place, settled on a table in the back corner, and sat with my back to the wall. I ordered some green tea, steeped not shaken, and informed the waiter I would order lunch when my comrade arrived. Toronto had a hip, cosmopolitan vibe. It was much different than the poverty-stricken region I had just explored in Cambodia. On an overhead flat screen, a CNN commentator was reporting about how Assad had accepted Frumpf's peace summit invitation. As I sipped on my scorching hot tea, I noticed an attractive platinum blonde woman enter. As she sashayed towards my table, it became rousingly apparent it was Thelma. She appeared to have dropped a few pounds, and was dressed in tight jeans and a white cashmere sweater. With not a trace of gray hair, she looked younger. I stood up so fast to greet her that I knocked over my tea. She just laughed and said,

"Down Boy."

Over lunch, we shared our tales of the road and the deep thoughts along the way. Although Stonehenge was eye opening, she was more taken by my Cambodian river experience. I was surprised she had been living in a house for a few days with Snopes and wondered how that all came about. I was fascinated to learn that Snopes was fully immersed in a romance with her cousin Rhoda.

When we arrived at Rhoda's, they were open armed. Snopes was a new man. It occurred to me that everyone involved in our drama was evolving in a positive direction. Everyone except me, the great dick decimator. Snopes was so relaxed, it was hard to remember that I was on the lam, wanted for treason by the president of the United States. Snopes had enlisted his daughter to housesit while he was gone, and follow his carefully written instructions on how to care for his coveted greenhouse creations. The atmosphere at Rhoda's was so festive I wished that Thelma and I didn't need to conceal our affection from her cousin who believed Thelma was still was Norman's gal.

While Rhoda and Thelma whipped up their version of a Canadian dining experience, Snopes and I discussed the recent political landscape and attempted to prophesize where this whole debacle was leading. He claimed Frumpf's approval rating is now the highest for any president, and his *Executive Zone* has turned out to be the greatest piece of political propaganda ever conceived. We discussed whether it was all a charade and if Frumpf was playing peacenik with the public to bask in the glow of the accolades while an ulterior motive incubated. We couldn't begin to predict whether or not he would be able to live the rest of his life without having sex, and joked that instead of an erection he would do it by getting a *zoner*. Pre-dinner cocktails turned into a fine supper of storytelling and naughty remarks. During dessert, which was a cake we were warned might have some gefilte fish properties, the topic of my mother came up, and the fascination regarding her being a shaman priestess. I went to my guestroom and retrieved one of the crystals I had been schlepping around in my bag. I put it on the table and said that somehow these translucent rocks hold ancient powers that are not fully understood. Rhoda asked if I could demonstrate its power.

Messing around with sacred entities while intoxicated was something I knew was taboo, but since we were all so chummy, tipsy, and loaded from the cake, I decided to at least be playful. I picked up the crystal and placed it against Thelma's forehead. I did my best guru impersonation and said the spirit of the lake demands that she transform her identity into the queen of seduction. Instead of laughing, which was what I was going for, Rhoda and Snopes stared at Thelma as if they were waiting for the spell to manifest. As I put the crystal back on the table, Thelma acted like she was in a trance, and began moving her chair closer to mine. She looked deep into my eyes, leaned forward, and gave me a one-minute passionate kiss on the lips. When she was done, she acted as if she'd snapped out of it, which then had Rhoda and Snopes in stitches. Now I was the one in a trance. Whatever magic occurred apparently also worked on Snopes and Rhoda who claimed it was time to "hit the hay." As they meandered off, Rhoda insisted we not bother attempting to do the dishes. Thelma and I moved to the couch where I admitted I was amazed at all the developments that were a direct result of our so-called mission.

"Your widowed cousin has found love, Snopes has found love, and you've transformed into a younger, different version of yourself," I said.

To this, she asked, "Have I also not found love?"

I pointed out that she had love to begin with, stressing whatever it is we shared was frivolous, undefined, and even somewhat of a personal dilemma. She told me that she does not have a dilemma. She claimed she would always love Norman, but the sanctum of intimacy where her heart now resides is impossible to desert. She added it was more than our sexual connection diverting her interest from her marriage. Her being was now on a journey of discovery, taking along her transformed consciousness that could never accept a life with a man who lives in fear, and who is content with the eternal 9 to 5. I was remiss to tell her that I have recently been terrified by just about everything, and instead I reminded her that Norman was instrumental in moving our plot forward. She joked by asking me whose side I was on. I told her as much as I enjoyed her company, her sexuality, her sense of adventure, and her new hair, I did not want to be responsible for breaking up her marriage, which could potentially ruin Norman's life. Thelma scolded me for not learning anything. As an example, she used Frumpf and the rash of unexpected developments that occurred due to my penile intervention.

She said, "Life is jam packed with many different chapters with unintended results."

Although I followed her logic, I interrupted, and asked where she was going with this, with us? Was she thinking about leaving Norman? Did she believe we knew enough about each other to take such a leap? What if I wound up with life in prison for treason, would she still be content with her divorce decision? The conversation had now reached a level of gloom Thelma wasn't willing to entertain, so she changed the subject to inform me that her room had a very special pillow she would like to introduce me to. God, she was good at getting what she wanted. On our way, she made a quick stop at my guestroom to rustle the blanket to make the bed looked slept in. She then took me by the hand and led me to a destination called inevitable.

World peace is the concept everyone wants you to believe was their birthday wish, even when it was really for a Tesla Model S. As the public celebrated the prospect of peace derived from Frumpf's global summit, which so far, has been more word than deed, there were those behind the scenes that were not delighted with the scenario. A consortium of rich corporate skunks, the head of the NRA, and key scoundrels of the Military Industrial Complex held their own summit in a remote warehouse. It was of their opinion Frumpf's newly fracked feminine side was antithetical to their world order agenda. They determined he needed his dick back, or at least some "cojones" as one puffy official added to chuckles from the menacing group. They came up with a 3-point plan. The first step was to read Frumpf the riot act and demand he backtrack on his bullshit unification rhetoric, maintaining more of a patriotic militarized regimen. If that didn't work, they needed to find the freak that castrated him to get him his balls back. They all knew what the third point was without saying, and hoped it wouldn't have to come to that.

World peace is a powerful concept, but not the type of powerful that should make it a threat to war hawks insulated by a nation's full militia. How insane is it that the loveliest practice there is could inspire officials to resort to assassination just to thwart it? Many citizens believe when a new president is sworn in he is met with a representative of the military *malefactory* who spells out the rules of what can and cannot be accomplished. If the president refuses to comply, it is believed the Cabal-Corp threatens to kill their wife or children, end of story.

Before their meeting adjourned they decided not to wait to see if Frumpf would adhere to their demand willingly, and consented to commence an all out search for the fucker who got them into this mess, *moi*.

*55

After five days of what felt like a dual honeymoon with Thelma and our hosts, Snopes was heading back to New York to handle household logistics. He was going to rent out his home, arrange for the transfer of his prized plants to Toronto, and relocate here where he and Rhoda planned to make a go of it. He also needed to check in with Frumpf to find out where he was regarding the future of his *Executive Zone*. Snopes was remiss about tearing himself away from his new love, especially when he experienced how much Rhoda was equally sad they had to temporarily part. When Rhoda was leaving to drive Snopes to the airport that evening, she told us not to bother unmaking the bed in the guestroom and winked.

Thelma shared she had heard from Norman who complained he was sad and lonely. She said he feels like he had lost her, and needed to see her. She confided although his sadness didn't induce guilt, she did feel bad for him. She went on to say that after the last few days of our sexual alliance, and deep communication she is sure she could never go back to the way life was. She changed the focus, and asked me about Lana, wondering about my feelings for her. She wanted to know if the sex with her was also amazing. The only response I could think of was that even when I was with Lana, I thought of Thelma constantly. I explained the whole tantric thing and even suggested we add that to our repertoire as well. Thelma concluded that if it weren't for the fact we were fugitives, she would go back to New York, and put her marriage to rest.

*56

Personally, although some take it way too far, I don't think there is anything freaky about neatness. When Snopes arrived home, his place was cleaner and more organized than he thought possible. Ella and Angela have systems, evidenced by the shoes in his closet that appeared to have been buffed. There was a note on the sparkling counter claiming that some very ominous guys in suits paid him a visit, and were intent on hearing from Snopes immediately. When he called the number using his now smudge-less landline, he got the Pentagon switchboard. Uninterested in traveling to Washington, Snopes arranged to meet these men at his temporary office at FBI headquarters. Whatever it is they wanted, he felt they would treat him with more respect if they remained aware he appeared to be on the same team.

At the meeting, they claimed that before they put Norman through the kind of interrogation you wouldn't wish on an enemy, they would check to see if Snopes knew how to locate me. After our camaraderie in Toronto, there was no way he would willingly turn me into guys that boasted of torturous interrogation. At the same time, he did not want to cause Norman to go through that kind of treatment, even though the truth about Thelma and me might kill him anyway. Snopes claimed that he needed to know what their plans were for me, as he was working on an agenda of his own. He needed to know if they were on the same page. The mouthpiece of the group bluntly said,

"We are going to get that guy to put Frumpf's dick back if we have to cut his off and superglue it to the president's crotch."

Snopes said although he didn't have quite the same plan, the end results were similar and said he needed time. They gave him two days or as they so sweetly put it,

"Norman would experience Normandy."

Basking in his publically patronized penislessness and the popularity of his plagiarized peace promise, Frumpf was now about to engage in a summit of another kind. Under the carefully crafted guise of 'I have changed,' Frumpf appealed to his wife and daughter to participate in a shared session with Idsel Cohen. His pitch was that no matter what they have decided about him, it was the least they could do to handle the situation responsibly. Frumpf was walking a thin line because he wasn't sure the first lady was even aware of Valina's molestation allegations, but felt Idsel was the key to mediating Frumpf back into a close relationship with his family.

When the ladies arrived, Idsel suggested Frumpf come out from behind his desk and sit near them so as not to exude an atmosphere of hierarchy. Frumpf complied, approached the women, and gave them both a squeeze on the hand. Idsel laid down the ground rules saying "Richard" was going to speak first, and the ladies would each have an uninterrupted chance to respond if they so desired. Idsel determined that calling the president by his first name would help humanize him a bit more. Frumpf began by apologizing from the bottom of his heart for anything he did to break their trust. He said he was overwhelmed by profound events, and got lost in a sea of self-involvement. He addressed his wife and pointed out she was well aware he never really thought he would win the presidency, and it was an outcome that shocked them both. He tried to be humorous by saying his old mindset would have been to sue the voters for getting him into this. No one was laughing. He then said he had learned a lot, and hoped it wasn't too late for them to recognize his positive evolution, and give him another chance. He ended by saying he loved them both more than anything in the world.

After Idsel had confirmed Frumpf was done, he asked the ladies if they wanted to respond. Valina began to speak. She told her father that although she was happy to see him aspire to grow and appeal to the compassionate needs of the public, she didn't think she could ever trust him. She said he remained in denial about his actions toward her as a child, which was something she could not heal while feeling like Frumpf thought it was an overblown fabrication. The look on Teresa's face became more severe, as this was the first she had heard about these allegations.

Valina continued by saying Frumpf will always be her father, but until the day comes where she can rationalize forgiveness, she no longer wanted to spend time with him alone or share her private life with him in any way. Frumpf began to interrupt but was stopped by Idsel who insisted he comply with the rules of this engagement. Valina announced she was done.

Idsel asked Teresa if she cared to speak. She nodded yes, and addressed Frumpf by saying he has always been a despicable man. She said when she was younger she foolishly equated his opulence with success. She said she abhors his touch, and admitted that when they had sex, she would think of anyone but him. She looked at Valina, and confided to her stepdaughter there were many occasions where Frumpf would ask her to pretend she was Valina while they had intercourse. She apologized and claimed at the time she had no idea it went beyond fantasy. She looked Frumpf right in the eyes and said she hoped he continued to fight for peace, rights, and the betterment of humanity, even though she was doubtful even all of that would be enough to clean his karma from his con artist past.

When Idsel was satisfied all had been said he recommended everyone now spend time with their feelings and let them process for a few days. Frumpf suddenly felt a pang in his crotch. It was almost as if a hidden dick was trying to break out to help him lash back. He erupted into verbal flames, damning them both for not giving him a chance. He went on to list all the things he had given them; homes, vacations, schools, cars, jewelry. He insisted they were being selfish, and that he deserved the right to prove himself. In a symbolic gesture, Teresa removed her pearls, laid them on the table, and insisted he did just prove himself. She bid Valina and Idsel farewell as she exited. Valina motioned for her to wait, took off her diamond bracelet, placed it on the table next to the pearls, and left with Teresa.

Frumpf looked over at Idsel and said,

"That went well."

58

Norman, Norman, Norman. The somber message from Snopes regarding retrieving me, or causing Norman to be tortured put a damper on things. As much as Thelma professed being ready for a divorce, she was equally alarmed at the prospect of her husband being water-boarded to find out where I was hiding. My discussion with Snopes delved deeper into the controversy, as I tried to unravel my future in the custody of these gun-loving miscreants. Especially after they deemed I was unable to rectify the president's condition. Snopes refused to go there, and instead claimed he had a plan that takes into account the mystic tales of my journey. He told me to hang tight until he got back to me tomorrow.

Snopes set up a meeting at St. Patrick's Cathedral with the Cabal-Corp. They were reluctant to meet there, but he said it was essential in understanding his strategy to fix, or in this case un-fix Frumpf. When the three members of the group arrived, Snopes was seated in the front pew. After the initial chatter, he took a poll asking which of them considered themselves religious. They looked to each other, glanced up at the nearby statue of crucified Jesus, and all confirmed they believed in God. Snopes said if they believed in God, that also meant they believed in miracles. He said undoing Frumpf's dilemma was no short of a miracle, and it would require taking him to three international sites; Stonehenge, Lourdes, and the Stung Kbal Spean River in Cambodia. When they asked Snopes how he could be sure these sites were essential, he claimed it took a lot of research, and he was almost positive it would do the trick. Of course, in reality, he had no clue as to the possibility, but what he was sure of was it would take some time to arrange such an itinerary with Frumpf, and in the meantime, it would take the immediate heat off of Norman and me.

The Cabal-Corp told Snopes they would get back to him, but did not appear to be convinced. To them, it was a lot of international moving parts. Their problem though, was unless they dealt with Frumpf's condition, his softening might continue, and lead to a "shit-hole" of political concerns. While they decided, Snopes convinced Rhoda to spend time with him at his home while he prepared it to rent. Norman went on missing Thelma with no idea he was on the verge of the double whammy of torture and divorce. He certainly had no idea Thelma and I were now shacked up in Rhoda's house, engaging in wanton behavior like it was the end of time, which could be the case.

When the Cabal-Corp informed Frumpf of Snopes' plan, he too wanted to know how he could have ascertained it would be the cure. They had to admit it was an odd plan to make up out of thin air, which gave it some credibility in their minds. The Cabal-Corp was also extremely intent on returning Frumpf to his old ways, so they didn't see why it wasn't at least worth a try. A week later, Snopes was informed the arrangements were being made to follow through with the plan. At this point, Snopes had arranged to fly us back to the states to concoct the next level of this improvisational scheme. Norman was ecstatic to see Thelma. I accepted Snopes' lodging invite, as camping in little Brucie Timinsky's bedroom was hard enough without the fact Norman was about to have his heart broken.

*59

Thelma could not see sleeping next to Norman after the amount of time she had now been intimately involved with me. In the beginning, it was as if she had done a naughty thing, but now we were full blown lovers with an emphasis on full blown. Norman was more understanding than Thelma imagined and claimed from the very beginning of their relationship he thought his days were numbered, but decided any amount of time he got to spend with her was worth it. This, of course, hit Thelma right in the heart. It would have been much easier had he been angry or vindictive, but how do you not feel guilty abandoning 'sweetness'? Thelma said she wanted him to keep the house, and would only take half of their savings, which was around $15,000, to keep her going until she figured something out. Norman then asked if she was in love with me. Thelma confessed this whole presidential mission brought up parts of her psyche she longed to be in touch with, and now could never ignore. She said she would always have love for Norman, and softly voiced her hope they could remain family. She said she was about to participate in a scheme that would probably only prolong her freedom, and insinuated her future was very tentative. He told her to be careful and gave her a warm hug. With many tears, but little remorse, Thelma Timinsky walked out the door of the home she once coveted, and headed straight back to me with an open-winged heart.

*60

I couldn't complain about the tedious debriefing Snopes put me through regarding the three locations he told the Cabal-Corp were necessary to rectify Frumpf's problem, because not only was he trying to save the president's penis, but he was also attempting to save my ass. With Stonehenge, we determined that the pillars representing large sturdy cocks spoke for themselves. I was to try and re-enact the process that allowed me to reverse their perceived disappearance. If step one were mystical in any way, Frumpf would have more faith in the rest of the plan. Next on the list was the Lourdes grotto in France. Since most people arrive at the culmination of a pilgrimage, we would insist that we begin the visit from five miles away, forcing him to hike all the way there. This would give Frumpf and me ample time to bond in the beautiful countryside, or if we were lucky, it would cause him to drop dead. My job was to try and forge a friendship with the fucker to increase our chance for mercy when the whole thing failed. The final phase was the river of carved stone *phallics*, which was the perfect theme to top off the ruse. *Holy water flowing over ancient rock penises to embolden his crotch to re-hatch his original cock.* This would sound perfectly cosmically logical to anyone. We would insist there could be no Secret Service, and he would have to be in a master disguise throughout the journey so no one would recognize him.

As we hashed out the logistics, we both sighed and realized we were about to enact this whole extravagant charade simply to buy time. Before this chapter in my life, I felt like I had all the time in the world. There were many days where I had absolutely nothing to do and often forced myself to engage with the public just to feel vital. Snopes brought up our exit strategy when this whole thing ends in failure. We would somehow have to figure out a way to vanish into the Cambodian jungle without tripping off landmines. Thelma said it sounds like it's going to end like her and Louise, making reference to the film where the two women decide to drive off of a cliff rather than face the law for their wild deeds.

It was possible that the oval office was shaped that way so the president could give everyone the runaround. Frumpf summoned Snopes to meet him there to discuss the new strategy. When he arrived, it was not only Frumpf but Idsel, as well. Frumpf enlisted the therapist's presence because he wanted another opinion regarding our plan. He claimed the guys that are pushing him to move forward with this were not his usual trusted advisors' but members of the militarized faction he has recently appeared to suppress. Idsel suggested maybe they have another motive to get me involved in this so-called cure. Why would the Military Industrial Complex be so enthusiastic about something that appears so far-fetched? Snopes hadn't realized that the Cabal-Corp wasn't sent by Frumpf himself, which gave him new concern. He should have guessed that a guy who wants his dick back would think twice about sending henchmen threatening torture. Realizing the game was somewhat changed Snopes amended his resolve. He told them the chances of success were remote, but possible. He shared my cosmic experience at Stonehenge, plus the story about seeing Frumpf's image on the wall of the grotto at Penis River. He asked Frumpf if he had noticed anything different lately. Frumpf admitted he has been experiencing a pulsating down there that felt like he had a phantom cock. To lighten the mood Snopes said,

"Now there's an opera you may want to miss."

Frumpf turned to Idsel for feedback about the plan. The doc claimed that at this time it was Frumpf's only option, so it didn't matter what he thought. Frumpf asked Snopes to write up the exact scenario and not leave out even a comma.

The Statue of Liberty had always been the icon of welcome to people from all over the world. A gift from France depicting a Roman Goddess it was a three-dimensional statement of unbiased immigrant embrace. The Frumpf administration added a fourth dimension, which was a layer of hatred towards Muslims who had been carelessly stereotyped as sword-wielding terrorists. During his campaign, Frumpf promised retaliation that his racist worshippers thrived on. When citizens are destitute of sense and cents, they find solace in an external evil. It is easier to accept one's joblessness, and disposition is the fault of immigrants as opposed to one's own lack of initiative, or bullish adherence to an antiquated vocation. Which is why Frumpf also promised to reignite the coal industry. It was a lie that gave the strong of arm and weak of mind false hope. On this day I was more interested in the Lady's torch as I needed enlightenment. When I reached the observational platform, I gazed out over New York Harbor. Unarguably one of the most celebrated cities in the world, New York is a melting pot of community flavors. If opinions were gold, New York was the Fort Knox of perspective.

I thought about the word conviction and how it had a dual meaning for a reason; the awful beliefs that are too often branded in our minds can lead to a sentence of lifelong self-imprisonment. We think backward. Everyone should lead with love and then set out to achieve our goals glossed with solicitude. Instead, the masses set out to achieve love through consumptive bargaining and ruthless ambition. Our adherence to the illogical concept of sovereignty, an idea designed by kings and hierarchy, divides a world that should be sharing its resources instead of destroying them. By robbing the president of his reproductive apparatus, have I created my own form of supremacy? Did I become an obstacle in the order that is born through chaos? When I imagine I would sacrifice my life in exchange for world peace am I suffering from delusions of grandeur to think the longevity of my existence has any negotiable value at all? Somewhere in my heart, I realized that unless I come to terms with the fact that I may have wrongly deputized myself as God, I would not be able to reverse Frumpf's spell.

I also need to come to terms with the fact that I am now committing my life to Thelma. In the name of human decency do I have a responsibility to Norman? Of course, this question would have been better asked before I co-opted his wife's sexuality and turned her into my faithful partner in treasonous crime. As an endless barrage of ethical questions swirled through my mind, Lady Liberty seemed to turn her head towards me as if she was going to chime in. Already accustomed to the improbable activity of inanimate props during my meditative meanderings I just listened for her words:

"We would all like to believe we have a divine purpose. I was designed to inspire freedom and acceptance. Millions of fascinated souls have clambered up my loins as if the climb also included permanent spiritual ascension. For a couple of hours, people from all over the world use their admiration of my stature to validate their commitment to universal acceptance. They fool themselves into believing they are cleansed of their prejudice merely due to their proximity to my image. This is the same as believing you are a great lover after masturbating to porn. Icons are great reminders of the things they represent, but wearing a t-shirt depicting my likeness does not mean unbiased racial tolerance is etched in one's heart."

A group of camera-toting Japanese tourists joined me on the platform, and all greeted me with a bowing gesture. I looked back at Lady Liberty whose head was now turned back towards the view. I noticed one of the tourists wore a T-shirt that said,

"Make love Not War."

63

Creating the detailed report Frumpf had requested regarding the logistics of our journey back to dickfullness kept Snopes busy. He asked me to help him brainstorm. When I read his outline, I told him my intuition told me the only thing that mattered was the phallic-laced river in Cambodia. I said the spiritual scavenger hunt preceding it could be anything we make it. Not letting on about my recent Lady Liberty lip service I added,

"Hell, we can get him to discuss racial tolerance with the Statue of Liberty if we want."

Snopes loved the concept of a spiritual scavenger hunt and wondered where I came up with the outlandish idea of the Statue of Liberty discussion. As far as I was concerned, all spiritual icons were there to give clues to lead us back to the source so we might as well milk the concept, and give El Presidente an experience that at the very least would leave him with an exposure to something he clearly cares nothing about, but should. Snopes suggested that Rhoda, Thelma, and I, join him that evening in a gefilte fish induced planning session to see what we could conjure up. He also decided to invite his daughter Ella and Angela.

When we were all gathered in the living room, Snopes lead the orientation. When he explained to Ella and Angela the history of our plight, and detailed what we were currently up against, they were partially shocked, somewhat intrigued, but finally understood Snopes' recent vanishing penis passion. When he told the girls they were about to ingest spiked gefilte fish, Angela could not stop laughing. She said,

"Imagine you get arrested and put in prison, and you ask your cellmate what they're in for. They say murder, then they ask you, you hesitate, and then say gefilte fish."

Everyone laughed. They then devoured a healthy portion of the culinary cannabis. The first part of the discussion involved the less creative logistics of the plan; who would get to go? What kind of disguise would Frumpf need to wear? What happens when it doesn't work? One thing they decided was I would claim the penis regeneration could take a few days to a month so when it doesn't work Thelma and I have plenty time to disappear.

It was obvious when the fish began to take effect because there was more laughter, and folks began to forget what they were about to say. Snopes had made an outline of journey points to be discussed so we could stay on track. The first thing on the list was an overall concept. I dug in and said,

"It's to take the president on a spiritual scavenger hunt that will culminate in the Cambodia river of carved rock cocks where he will be led to believe that the holy waterfall will drench his being and cause the regeneration of his private parts."

When I was finished, everyone stared at me for a second and broke out in laughter. Thelma said she was impressed I could say all that with a straight face. When Snopes asked if anyone had anything to add, his daughter said,

"How could you possibly add to that?"

The second thing on his list was the question of security. How were they supposed to take the most famous figure in the world right now on a secret sojourn? The disguise, which garnered every playful suggestion from Zorro to Batman, wound up with a unanimous vote on "Hippy" with a longhair wig, beard, and mustache, bandana, etc. Everyone thought that image would meld well with the thematic journey, and what a coup to get Frumpf to dress in peacenik attire.

Everyone performed their impression of the commander in chief as a hippy.

"Hey dude, you know where I could cop some Agent Orange sunshine," said Thelma.

"I'll tell you what I am going to do about the homeless, they can all crash at my pad," said Ella.

"Anyone know where I can buy some good antacid," said Angela.

"It's not the destination, it's the limo," said Rhoda.

My impression was just the reversal of the t-shirt I had seen at the Statue of Liberty.

"Make war, not love," I said, but I could see by the look in Thelma's eyes that she soon planned on reversing it back again.

Every time the session headed for total comedic chaos, Snopes reeled it back in with the next item on his list. After a few hours, Ella and Angela said they needed to go, but had a blast. Ella, who was a bit reserved when she noticed Rhoda and her dad were now an item, eventually warmed up to her. When Snopes witnessed their bonding, he saw the flicker of a new family generating that nourished his spirit.

*64

The slang expression "far out" came to mind earlier as Snopes reviewed the game plan he was about to lay on Frumpf. The president was now reading the report while Snopes sat on the oval office couch watching his facial expressions for signs of disaster. When Frumpf was done, he put the pages down on his desk and asked if Snopes was on drugs when he wrote it. Snopes knew Frumpf wasn't being perceptive but was simply commenting about the outlandishness of the plan.

"You want me to disguise myself as a fucking Hippy?" Frumpf asked.

Snopes explained there was no way to accomplish the tranquility necessary to evoke the sacred results if there was a circus of gawkers surrounding us. He said anyone cruising with Secret Service would be suspect, so his disguise would only work in an innocuous environment. When Frumpf asked why the magic needed such quiet exclusivity when its initial spell was originally going to be cast during a rally of thousands, Snopes' said the reversal had different requirements, and he shouldn't mix logic with magic.

Frumpf stated,

"We should do the exact opposite. Make it an international event. Allow the masses in on the process. Have it covered by the media. Let the world witness the return of the presidential penis, which he described as the most monumental television event of all time. We could make it a reality show, pay-per-view."

"Or peepee-view," I responded, hiding my discontent.

When Snopes relayed the news, my first reaction was negative. It felt like another example of the governmental elite capitalizing on the sacred. Corporatizing national parks, dangerous oil pipelines through Native American waters, commercializing the coastline. But another thought came over me; this may be a chance to teach the world the value of meditation. A way to enhance spiritual connection and respect for the environment by illustrating the magic possessed in ancient natural habitats. The more I thought about it, the more appealing it became. We would no longer have to deal with the logistics of a clandestine charade. It would be a shameless presidential pilgrimage back to penis. Then it hit me:

All the media hype and attention would turn me into a mega-celebrity I did not want to be.

After a surprise sex attack by Thelma, she said she had an idea to propose. She and Rhoda had gone shopping for Hippy stuff to begin designing a look for Frumpf. She claimed maybe I should be the one disguised as the hippy, only take it further and make me a guru. She enjoyed dressing me up, and I had to admit that once decked out in the 60s garb, with full facial hair, I hardly recognized myself. Thelma entered the kitchen where Rhoda was teaching Snopes how to bake a cake. She commanded their attention by announcing that she wanted to introduce her new friend. She pulled me into the room and with the utmost fanfare said,

"Lady and gentleman. Allow me to introduce **Baba Dickster**."

At first, they didn't know it was me behind the beard, but as my familiar facial expressions gave way it became obvious. Snopes let out a big guffaw regarding the name Thelma gave me confirming my destiny. The three of them were so enthusiastic that I decided to consider this outlandish change of identity. It was Thelma's notion we create a book, so we could capitalize on the exposure generating enough money to hide away somewhere exotic forever. Although commercialization was something I usually did not resonate with, I did see this as an opportunity to amass funds we could also put towards the betterment of the planet. I already had pages and pages of notes and sketches I had journaled throughout this whole experience that would be easy to organize into a marketable treatise.

65

"The Presidential Penis Pilgrimage" was confirmed to commence in thirty days. Frumpf insisted he now needed to meet with me. Snopes agreed but claimed it would have to be as Baba Dickster. He said the media did not know the man who rescued Frumpf was the same guy who castrated him. If I were to have any future, it would have to remain that way. Frumpf asked why he should give a shit about my future after I did what I did to him. Snopes reminded him I also saved his life and am about to undo the curse.

Although the Washington monument was not quite a spiritual setting, its obelisk design made it the perfect symbol of phallic prospect. Rhoda had suggested we do a teaser and film the first meeting between Frumpf and Dickster at the monument. The area was closed off to tourism that evening, and famed director Spike Penn was commissioned to film the encounter. To give it the ethereal touch, two large Turkish pillows were placed facing each other on a Persian rug with a variety of phallic candles and crystals littering the site. Personally, I thought the penis candles they found at a sex shop were a bit much, but Snopes thought it would sell the concept. What we both loved was with a rug from Iran and pillows from Turkey, Frumpf was blindly endorsing a Muslim atmosphere.

The president was filmed arriving in the executive limo. He was greeted by Rhoda, who looked exotic in a silk robe and feather laced hairdo. She escorted him to his pillow, ignited a sage smudgy using a candle, and anointed Frumpf with ceremonial smoke. Spike was filming this hand-held and was extremely pleased with the irony of the scene. Then, appearing from behind the monument was the most elegantly adorned hippy anyone has ever seen. As Baba Dickster, I made a grand entrance next to Thelma who was undeniably a platinum-haired goddess. My long hair was flaked with turquoise glitter, and my bandana had an emerald stone in the center. I was wearing a suit that was faintly embossed with the OM symbol, a spiritual icon of the Hindu religion, and wore leather sandals that exposed my toenails, which were painted with a translucent silver hue. Thelma escorted me step by step to the pillow opposite Frumpf. Rhoda anointed my whole body with the sage smoke, as I reclined into a lotus position on the pillow.

Spike was ecstatic about the opening procession. As I sat there silently staring at Frumpf, the dickless leader seemed bewildered, and unsure of how to deal with the feelings he was experiencing being part of something this bizarro. When Spike brought the camera close, I asked the president if he was ready to take a journey inside. He said he was. I asked him if living without his penis had taught him anything beneficial. He said it had. I asked for his hands and held them in mine while I went into a momentary trance. When I opened my eyes, I told him I felt he was ready, and that his ensuing change was going to be more than physical because he would also instill peace into the anatomy of the planet. Sitar music emanated from a musician leaning against the monument. Rhoda and Thelma ceremoniously blew out all the candles one by one. We were done.

When Spike's edited version hit the airwaves, it went viral. All the news stations, every talk show showed the two-minute clip. It had 20 million hits on YouTube. The late night monologues couldn't get enough;

Jimmy Fallon: "Earlier this week President Frumpf met with Guru Baba Dickster who is going to help him get his penis back. Part of Frumpf's plan to "Make America Mate Again."

Stephen Colbert: "I'm sure everyone has seen the segment by now. President Frumpf meeting with Baba Dickster. If it doesn't work, Frumpf claims the vice president will have to step in to screw the country for him."

Jimmy Kimmel: "Looks like President Frumpf is relying on a Guru, Baba Dickster, to help him get his genitalia back; if this works I hear he may hit up the Wizard of Oz to find him a heart.

Since my true identity was not known the press could not locate me. They tried every trick in the book, but even computerized face recognition didn't come up with a match. In all the past interviews Frumpf joked not only didn't he know where I was from, but also he wasn't even sure it was this planet, which the tabloids turned into: PRESIDENT FRUMPF CONFIRMS THE EXISTENCE OF ALIEN BEINGS ON EARTH.

Ella and Angela took on the great task of transforming my notes into a book.

ANATOMIX by Baba Dickster, A GUIDE TO RECLAIMING YOUR SPIRITUAL CORE, was on par with any other self-help book, except ours was going to have a shot of the president and me surrounded by penis candles on the cover.

Everything was happening so fast there wasn't time to predict the pitfalls. Thelma became obsessed with our new personas and insisted we remain in character during our ongoing sexual escapades. There was no argument from me as her Goddess garb was overly enticing.

As the days went on you couldn't turn on the television without seeing a reference to Baba Dickster. There was the usual Christian repudiation claiming Dickster was the devil, and we should not allow our country's leader to give into the temptation of this black magic.

*66

To the disappointment of many, Idsel Cohen announced his retirement from his therapy practice. Thirty years was enough, and recent events made him realize it was time to quit. The pressures put on him by Frumpf made him realize the world has changed. Although the classic themes that induce people to seek therapy haven't changed, the level of discontent, and ability to process his form of treatment had. He no longer felt passion for his practice. When he informed the president, Frumpf congratulated him but said he was glad Idsel would continue to counsel him. When Idsel told him it was working with Frumpf that inspired him to retire, Frumpf felt blamed and reacted by accusing Idsel of being a loser. Frumpf claimed that he would sign an executive order requiring government therapists to need permission from their patients to retire. But when Frumpf realized normal methods of manipulation are wasted on a man who has seen it all, he altered his stance and begged him to stick with him until the Penis Pilgrimage was over. Since it was only a few weeks away, Idsel agreed.

When Idsel notified Valina about his retirement, she was distraught. To her, it was as if her best friend, closest family member, key confidant, and lifeline suddenly died. Instead of lashing out, she asked him how she was supposed to deal with her daddy issue now. She claimed there was no way she could start the process all over with someone else, especially because of the sensitive nature of her situation. Idsel loved Valina like a daughter, so her justifiable anxiety touched his heart. How does a therapist ever quit? Unless Frumpf had his way, there is no part of their oath that demanded he remain a doctor for life. Sure there are replacement therapists as good as him, but it would take a long time to build up the trust and understanding patients like Valina had developed. Idsel told her the problem with parental molestation matters was they were almost impossible to heal, which is why they are so harmful. But in his professional opinion, he didn't believe Frumpf completely crossed the line.

He told her a story about a time he and his wife were in a museum in Paris visiting a lovely photo exhibit in one of the galleries. He claimed that on the wall were photos of a family; a young couple and two young kids. In the exhibit, the family was completely naked posing with the children on their laps, etc. He said that the visitors were not only okay with the photos, but it uplifted them in a very sweet, non-sexual way. Idsel said an exhibit like that in America would have landed the parents in prison. He told her he believed her father had one of the worst traits a human can possess, excessive narcissism. He said the president is not capable of seeing beyond his own needs and has his own set of rules and standards that reduce him to the behavior of an adolescent. Idsel said he was convinced that the only way she will heal from her father's self-serving arrogance was to find it in her heart to forgive him. He added that Frumpf is a product of his dad's misguidance, as his dad was of his dad, and on and on for generations. Somewhere along this lineage, someone has to break the dysfunctional chain, he explained. As Valina stared at him with her teary eyes, Idsel encouraged her to spend the next couple of weeks processing this, and if she still wanted to talk after that he would make time for her. He insisted he was in no way excusing underage improprieties, but believed in her dad's case it was a very blurry line. He also added that he and his wife would like to include her in their lives, and though he was closing the door of his office, he was not shutting the portal to his heart.

*67

Since all of the travel arrangements and security measures for the Penis Pilgrimage were being handled by the White House, the book was ready to launch on Amazon, and the initial publicity had been done, Thelma and I decided to give Snopes and Rhoda space so they could get his house rented and relocate to Canada. We offered our help, but Rhoda suggested since we were about to face a stressful, uncertain future we should take a vacation somewhere, and polish our bond. Thelma appreciated the thoughtfulness and suggested we go somewhere all-inclusive like a Club Med to unwind. Turns out Rhoda's college roommate married a guy who managed a sustainable, luxury bush camp in Zambia, Africa. Thelma admitted that for an international fugitive she was not that adventurous when it came to lions, tigers, and bugs, vying for more of a Kurt and Goldie experience than a Tarzan and Jane. I told her I doubted Tarzan's plunge pool was filtered or Jane's bed was lined with raw linen. I expressed that due to the stressful nature of our upcoming pilgrimage I would love to visit a place where the call of the wild is all that breaks the silence, and I doubted that the vacation oriented all-inclusive type of resorts would fit that bill. After looking at the photos and list of amenities, it was clear to Thelma the place Rhoda suggested offered us the best of both worlds. She appreciated that we would have the privacy and tranquility to chill before the pilgrimage. It was also a place where even if the world caught on to who I was they would never be able to approach us until we returned. I finalized my pitch by telling her it is an exotic atmosphere where the glow of the setting sun would enhance the drum beat of our hearts, and inspire us to let each other fall deeper into the abyss of devotion. She claimed I had her at raw linen.

*68

While Snopes and Rhoda were boxing up Snopes' life, the Cabal-Corp paid him a visit. Not wanting Rhoda exposed to their odious energy, he ushered them off to a neighborhood park. The four of them sat together at a cement table often used by the locals to play chess. They wanted to know why Snopes altered the original pilgrimage plan. He explained that Frumpf insisted it go down like this, giving him little choice, and he thought the revision was their doing so he avoided making waves. The shorter fat guy wasn't pleased and claimed the alteration could potentially make matters worse for them as people think guru stuff has to do with world peace. Snopes had to respect them for one thing; they never lost sight of their agenda. Maybe it was from proofreading my upcoming book, or his renewed sense of family that made Snopes declare the following,

"Don't you guys have any other ways of feeding your greed without making the rest of civilization suffer? Can't you turn war into a game where you're rewarded for preserving the most lives instead of destroying them? Don't you breathe the same fucking air you're polluting with your insane military aspirations?"

The three of them were not used to being berated, and except for the fact they do breathe the same air their answer to all the other questions was "no." War was not only a way to steal other country's resources, but a method of population control they deemed natural. Snopes realized that he was addressing extremists that were involved in arming both sides of many wars; so appealing to their compassion was like asking a cockroach to sing. There was only one man whose voice garnered their undivided attention, their accountant, and he claimed ever since Frumpf's penis problem surfaced they have seen a decline in trends that have kept their coffers overflowing. Snopes was disgusted and informed them if they want to change the pilgrimage they would have to deal with Frumpf himself.

*69

When the indigenous folks of Zambia talk about the smoke that thunders they are referring to Victoria Falls. Thelma kept repeating she could not believe she was sitting there. "I can't believe this" became Thelma's mantra as we explored Africa's wildlife infested national parks, and rainforests that instead of being drenched by the rainclouds were watered by the constant mist of the falls. Each time Thelma said, "I can't believe this" I would say,

"Then believe in it, because you will never forget it."

Hippos, leopards, hyenas, elephants, monkeys, apes, were not just wildlife to Thelma, they were another life, one she never dreamed of ever experiencing. She was so enamored by the enchanted scenery that she reminded me of a child witnessing her first snow, or rainbow. Our accommodations were living proof of the kind of luxury that could be had when a creative, soulful eye has an abundance of natural elements to choose from. There were a few moments when she reflected back to her honeymoon with Norman in Madrid, where they attended bullfights that made her cringe and dined while watching flamenco dancers that made her dream of being someone else; someone she felt she now was.

Thelma's consciousness was like a sponge for the sanctity of nature, and it felt like she was now witnessing it all through the eyes of love. Our sex that night was different but by no means inferior. Our need for wildness was tempered by the wilder terrain, and our physical prowess was no match for the grace of the local fauna. That night Thelma became tantric. Her orgasms were being nurtured through her heart. As we were safely nestled under thick mosquito netting in one of the most exotic locations in the world, Thelma looked into my eyes and said,

"I want to stay here with you for the rest of our lives."

Thelma's request wasn't a bad idea for many reasons. I really didn't want to go through with the whole Dickster charade. It would eventually come out it was Baba Sheldon, a nobody loner with a rape inspired penis spell, who momentarily thought it was my place to save the world. And did I? The *Executive Zone* has now not only popularized an arrogant misogynist, but has added a blank crotch to the list of alternative porn choices. Transgenders revered me for my cock erasing magic, and if the penis pilgrimage is successful dykes will seek me out to endow them for real. It didn't matter because I have extreme doubts the pilgrimage had any chance of giving Frumpf back his privates. There is no precedent to suggest I could do it, and my best hope of a future is that Thelma and I use the potential book royalties to sneak off into the global ether.

Throughout my life I have always been jealous of people that are born with special gifts; piano virtuosos, math masters, that kid who can draw full cities in detail by memory, and I doubt any of them would trade their exceptional talent in for the ability to erase genitalia. I'm not a prodigy; I'm a freaking walking weenie guillotine. Why was I even given this penis version of alt control delete? I could have just as easily knocked my mother's rapist out with the wand until the cops arrived, instead of becoming a bewildered witch doctor with a secret too dark to tell. I don't even know what happened to my first target. I had trouble sleeping for many years worrying he might return to force me to put it back. God, whoever or whatever you are, if you can hear my thoughts let me hear yours in return. Give me a respectable reason why I have been chosen to possess such a bizarre ability. Give me the magic to reverse the spell. Then relieve me of this talent.

Thelma and I took in every site, hike, and activity the guides from our Zambia resort had to offer. From the crocodiles along the Luangwa river to the nocturnal porcupines. Thelma took thousands of photos and insisted that although I was right about her never forgetting the trip, she was taking no chances on forgetting one second of what we saw. We were thrilled to have been there for the full moon over Zambia. The contrasting shadows on its face made it look more three-dimensional than usual. A few nights later Thelma and I wandered a bit further out of the camp than advised, and it began to get dark. As we headed back, Thelma suddenly froze her step and became rigid. Right in front of her was the epitome of the jungle, the King of it all. I immediately told her not to panic. She said I was a little late and every cell of her being was on alert. She asked if we should run, to which I said "definitely not," unless she could sprint sixty miles an hour. He was the classic male lion of the MGM logo. It turns out lions count on the days after the full moon to have darkness in the early evenings for a few hours to seek prey. I told

Thelma the fact his tail was swishing was a good sign in that it means he was contemplating more than hunting. She asked what the lion was contemplating, to which I replied

"Hopefully prey he passed along the way."

I told Thelma—whose eyes tried to vacuum the tears back into the ducts so the animal wouldn't perceive her fear—we need to slowly back away, and if the lion moves forward, we should freeze. "Trust Me," I whispered, even though I sensed at least one of us was about to become dinner. I would do anything I could to make sure it was me. After taking ten very slow steps back, the lion moved forward. Thelma was using every bit of her self-control not to scream at the top of her lungs. The lion suddenly lunged forward in a mock attack. We were both so frozen in fear we didn't even flinch. The lion was closer now, and Thelma was quick to point out that his tail was no longer wagging. The next thing Thelma said was surprising. "Baba Dickster," she muttered. It took a few seconds for me to understand what she was inferring. She wanted me to try and make the lion's privates disappear. Although any method of survival was on the table, I doubted my power worked on animals, and even if it could, would stalking us count as being evil? To a lion we were either preventing it from getting food, threatening their cubs, or just a notch lower on the food chain. Through human eyes, the stalking of a wildebeest may seem barbaric, but in the eyes of nature, it's merely survival.

"You can do this," Thelma said. "That hungry beast is angry with us for shooting his fellow lions in the past, and he is here for fucking revenge. He isn't even hungry; he wants to rip your fucking body apart."

Thelma continued painting a portrait of the animal as a vindictive monster whose only motivation in life is murder. I had to momentarily suppress my usual love for all beasts, and go along with her ploy. As my eyes locked in a competitive stare with our stalker, his tail began to wave again, and he backed up a bit without looking away from my impending castrating glare. Then what felt like no less than a miracle, he turned away and ran off. Thelma swears I did a Dickster on him, but I think he sensed I thought I could so he passed on the confrontation. We wasted no time heading back to our room, spending the rest of the night cuddled, discussing "what ifs."

*70

Having shipped the boxes with his important belongings to Canada, and the house now leased for a year, Snopes and Rhoda took up temporary residence at a luxury D.C. hotel, paid for by the government. Frumpf insisted they remain close by during the last two weeks of planning and was a bit miffed when he heard Baba Dickster would be gone for a few more days. Frumpf had more riding on this than the retrieval of his penis. The media attention around the pilgrimage was the ultimate distraction for his administration's corruption, a detail about the production which none of us liked supporting. His peace summit rhetoric was short lived, and if the pilgrimage fell through for any reason, it would be seen as a stunt, causing his recent boost in rating to plummet faster than Flint Michigan real estate prices. Frumpf fed off of Snopes confidence in the Pilgrimage, a conviction based on nothing but blind faith in me. Everything was just smoke and mirrors until the final river ceremony when, as Snopes put it,

"You just abracadabra the president's dick right back again, then we circumcise our existence outa there."

I wish I had his optimism, and also sometimes wished he didn't have his.

71

The easiest way to add square footage to a home is to suddenly find yourself living there alone. With Thelma gone, every reminder of her existence enhanced the gloom in the room. So when his neighbor Sarah Epstein said she had an attractive, recently divorced friend, who was financially down on her luck, Norman invited her to move into the guest quarters. Pauline Castleman was the quiet, artistic type, and slowly began to transform Thelma's prosaic motif into more of a bohemian, colorful enclave. Pauline had an art degree from Pratt Institute in Brooklyn but had no aspirations outside of surrounding herself with creative ambiance. In lieu of rent, Pauline would take care of all of the household chores; even preparing sumptuous vegetarian dinners she would have waiting for Norman when he came home from work. Although they felt an instant kinship that distracted from their similar recent desolation of the heart, neither she nor Norman was ready to open up to something more. They were fine just to share the space, and remind each other that life goes on. It was a busy time for Norman as Flimsy Fork was about to launch their big infomercial.

During dinner, Norman told Pauline he met the famous infomercial personality, Don O'Neil. Norman said it was hard to believe, but O'Neil was more outspoken about himself and his accomplishments than he was about the products you see him hawking on TV. Don didn't need to promote any more gadgets as he was already worth millions, and had everything a man could want, except one thing he would never have, enough. He needed the continuous accolades to make him feel whole, not unlike many entertainers whose sun is the spotlight. No matter how dynamic a story someone told, O'Neil was able to one-up them. If a guy bragged about skydiving, O'Neil let on about how he bungee-jumped off of the space shuttle. But a man with a cultivated sense of the grandiose was the perfect person to turn an odd trinket like Flimsy Fork into,

"The revolutionary new weight loss device that will change your life, without changing your diet!"

If all went as planned Norman's company stock options would make him a wealthy man, a disclosure that made even minimalist Pauline a little more ready to love again than she thought.

72

When Thelma and I returned to New York from our death-defying, non-marital honeymoon we were homeless. My apartment was still there, but having never repaired the lock Snopes screwed up when he let himself in, my slummy neighbors helped themselves to the furnishings. After living in luxury on the edge of the Congo for ten days, the apartment would have been like residing in an empty closet anyway. Snopes' home was no longer available, so we were pleasantly surprised when Ella met us at the airport. Snopes informed her we had a suite reserved in their same D.C. hotel and asked if she could put us up for a night or two in New York when we arrived at JFK. As it turned out Angela had a little pied-a-terre they never used in Chelsea because they were living together at Ella's full time. We were warmed by Snopes' thoughtfulness and Chelsea it was. On the way to the apartment, Thelma could not stop talking about the lion experience. Ella barely got a word in edgewise. When we arrived at the hip little pad, Ella gave us a quick rundown and advised us where we could grab the tastiest bite nearby, then left us to unwind. After our fifteen-hour flight from Africa, the jet lag put us straight to sleep till the following afternoon. Snopes called informing us we needed to get to Washington immediately because Frumpf was completely on edge and needed reassurance from me all was in the flow. I promised Snopes we would fly out the following morning and he said he would have the White House secretary make the arrangements. Thelma and I were a bit disoriented being back in the buzzing city after our adventure in the wilderness. We strolled to a local Tex-Mex café Ella had mentioned and had tacos with some potent mango margaritas.

Our flight the next day didn't leave till one p.m. so Thelma ventured to her old house to retrieve some personal items, since we may never be coming back here again. When she arrived at the home and put the key in the door, someone opened it from the inside.   Thelma came face to face with Pauline, who perceptively said,

"You must be Thelma."

She based her assumption on the fact that Thelma was using a key to get in, and more so she recognized her from the famous wedding video she had watched while Norman was at work. When Thelma nodded affirmatively, Pauline claimed she looked much younger and more beautiful in person. Before Thelma even asked who she was, her eyes surveyed the new artsy décor of her home. Feeling a bit awkward Pauline introduced herself as Norman's roommate. She could tell Thelma wasn't sure what that meant and added,

"Roommate, as in he has his room and I have mine."

Thelma cracked a smile in appreciation of Pauline's attempt to ensure Thelma knew she and Norman weren't shacking up. Thelma continued to silently survey the transformed atmosphere of the home she and Norman had postponed their honeymoon to purchase. The same home where last she saw her son Brucie. Then the first words out of Thelma's mouth were,

"He's a good man, and deserves to be happy."

Pauline nodded in agreement. She said she had some things to attend to in her room, leaving Thelma alone to take care of whatever she came for. When Thelma entered the master bedroom, she immediately focused on the framed wedding photo of she and Norman on the dresser. When she opened her closet, nothing seemed touched, while at the same time nothing she touched seemed the same. As she filed through her hanging clothing everything from the style to the fabric was disparate of who she was now. The one item that resonated with her was an old leather motorcycle jacket that belonged to her deceased dad. Thelma reached into her dresser drawer and grabbed a few things that she dropped into her purse; a fancy silver lighter that had belonged to her chain-smoking mom, a couple of pairs of sunglasses, and a watch. She took down a box of photos from the closet shelf and extracted a few. She grabbed a small jewelry box and then headed out. Before leaving, she stopped by Pauline's room. She took the woman's hand, placed the house key in her palm, and softly closed her fingers around it. On her way out the door Thelma simply said,

"I like what you've done to the place."

73

In comparison, the flight to D.C. seemed like it took a few seconds, as opposed to the interminable jaunt Thelma and had I experienced on our return from Zambia. It was enough time though for her to fill me in on the arty transformation of her former residence, as well as the new lady of the house, Pauline. Had Thelma felt invaded and remorseful I would have fully understood, but she claimed after a few moments of adjustment that she felt relief knowing Norman was not alone and was experiencing a metamorphosis of his own. When I asked Thelma if she was going through one, she answered by using her hands to draw attention to the leather motorcycle jacket she was wearing and then me. She described the evolution she was experiencing as enormous and acknowledged that every day with me was like a mini-life in itself. She claimed that if we wind up incarcerated after a failed pilgrimage she will peer through the bars with no regrets.

A formal Frumpf lackey greeted us at the terminal and whisked us right to the hotel. We weren't even in the room twenty minutes when Snopes knocked on the door, welcomed us back, and insisted I get into my Baba garb to meet with the president.

Prescription drugs? Too much scotch? Drunk on power? Frumpf was blabbing a mile a minute about everything imaginable. His therapist retiring, Teresa serving him divorce papers, Valina cutting him out of her life, a joke about the vice president having to be the one to screw the country if Frumpf doesn't get his dick back, and he even claimed if the pilgrimage was not successful he might have to start a war with North Korea as a distraction. I reminded him that the best chance we have of the penis pilgrimage working was to try and wean him of his evil ways. I explained that threatening needless wars to save his reputation was definitely not genitalia generating. He ignored my lecture and informed us that the sites on our itinerary were secured for our visit. He boasted they were setting up dinners with the President of France, and the King of Cambodia. He said the fucking Queen of England turned him down, and he wanted to know why all of the women in his life were so negative towards him. Snopes doused his ego saying he could hardly consider Queen Elizabeth part of his life, to which Frumpf said,

"Yeah, well it takes more than an overrated Queen to get away with trumping Frumpf."

After his personal purge, Frumpf demanded reassurance from me that I could manifest the magic. He questioned if I had ever recovered a penis, and more importantly, would it be the same size as the one that vanished. He insisted he could not accept a mini-version. I confessed I have never reversed a spell, but know of victims who recovered completely intact, with no subtraction. I had no clue, but better he feared as few things as possible. I speculated further and told him that the positive things he did for the world in the next couple of weeks enhanced the chance of his dick coming back larger. To show he had a sense of humor about it, he picked up the phone and pretended to tell his secretary to close Guantanamo.

As the time for the pilgrimage grew closer, Frumpf insisted we meet every day. Fortunately, Snopes claimed I was deep in regenerative meditation to build up my power. Good one Snopes! Thelma pushed us to launch the book, presuming if we waited till the pilgrimage failed no one would buy a copy. Even though we finagled it so the pilgrimage results could take a month, why take chances? I wasn't sure if it was her dad's motorcycle jacket she now wore everywhere except to bed, and even there a couple of times, but Thelma was becoming a force to be reckoned with.

I was very apprehensive about the amount of attention the book release might garner, and turned down appearing on every show under the sun. I could not imagine myself impersonating a guru while being interviewed on national television, so instead, Thelma and I made a simple iPhone video and posted it on YouTube. After what seemed like a million takes we finally decided they all sucked but chose this one:

Hi. I'm Baba Dickster. My new book, Anatomix, will help you source the same core power capable of regenerating a president's genitalia. The magic is not in me; I am merely a conduit to help you control your own anatomy. Don't let your special area wind up in the Executive Zone. Check out Anatomix Today. Bless you all.

Snopes and Rhoda thought it was funny, but not impactful enough. They suggested doing at least a couple of talk shows. I said I would think it over, but by morning *Anatomix* had already sold a million copies. Something happens on Amazon when you achieve numbers like these, causing them to put a lot more effort into promotion. The news shows cited our astronomical sales numbers and broadcasted our little iPhone video. This book made us overnight millionaires with no end in sight. That weekend SNL did a skit where the host played me reading Frumpf to sleep with penis passages they made up in parody. Major publishers wanted the book under their umbrella. When I turned them down, they offered a multi-million dollar contract for my next book. Thelma said if through some miracle the pilgrimage works we could consider it. I couldn't fathom what a second book could be about. I joked I'd have to make a vagina disappear, to which Thelma added,

"Now that would really make Frumpf upset."

*74

Norman, Pauline, familiar faces from Thelma's political rally, and employees of Flimsy Fork made up the studio audience of a commercial taping.

A young girl on stage began to speak,

"Welcome everyone. I'm happy you're here, and you will be too when you see what we are about to present for the very first time. Would you please welcome the man who has made life simpler for so many in so many ways, Don O'Neil!"

As Don entered the stage, he thanked the young girl and waved to the audience as they applauded loudly. Don said,

"Thank you, Laura, and thank you, ladies and gentlemen."

Laura left the stage waving.

Don continued,

"As most of you know, weight loss is one of the hardest personal struggles in America today. The diet industry is a multi-billion dollar business. But what if I told you there is a way to improve your health, that's right, change your life without changing your diet..."

*75

A week away from the Penis Pilgrimage, every hotel in Amesbury, Lourdes, Siem Reap, and surrounding areas were booked solid. Frumpf insisted that the four of us travel and sleep on Air Force One. We weren't sure if that meant a bed or reclining seat, but we doubted any of us were going to get much rest until the extravaganza was complete. During lunch, Snopes got a call from Frumpf sounding irate, and demanding we meet with him immediately. Snopes tried to remind him of my need for solitude, but Frumpf said to cut the crap and get over there. Upon entering the oval office Frumpf's first words were,

"Eight fucking million?!"

Snopes and I remained silent. The media had been reporting the book sale numbers, and as unfathomable as it was our profit thus far was very close to Frumpf's number. He continued,

"Some fucking Guru. You guys are playing me for the con. Believe me I know a scam when I see one. Hell, I invented half of them. What gives you the right to make eight fucking million dollars on my handicap? By the time the Pilgrimage is over it will probably triple that, over twenty million bucks because you stole my freaking dick. And what the hell does it mean, *Anatomix*?"

I said *Anatomix* was a word we thought would represent the recharging of one's anatomy. Snopes claimed the book's original intent was not to get rich, but to sell the whole Baba Dickster concept. He said the fact it is doing great proves the public cares about Frumpf and swore I planned on using most of that money for charitable causes. Frumpf laughed and said,

"Charitable fucking causes? You think I was born yesterday?"

Though he did have the personality of an infant, pointing it out would be less than beneficial. Snopes cut him off, and warned that stopping the flow of what he called "compassionate cash" is exactly the kind of action Frumpf needed to avoid to ensure he reclaimed his dick.

"Oh, you are good Snopes," Frumpf told him.

I was in awe of Snopes' strategy, as I was sure Frumpf wanted to demand as much of a percentage as his little hands could grab. Snopes replied,

"Here's the deal, Sir. From the very beginning my interest in this mess has been to get to the bottom of it, which I have. I put myself on the line to help you recover something I believe you want back more than anything. You either have to lighten up and go along with this plan, or say the word and we are done. There is no way Baba here, will be able to stay on track when you keep sabotaging his spirit. So what's it going to be, Sir?"

Both Frumpf and I were surprised by the tone of his bravado statement. Frumpf relented and said,

"This better fucking work."

Personally I could not wait to do what Snopes claimed and donate royalties to causes in need, since Frumpf's administration cropped funding for the arts, Planned Parenthood, legal aid, and a list of other things almost as long as the line of Syrian refugees waiting for a new place to call home. Thelma insisted we wait till the pilgrimage is over, so we don't create any trail leading back to us. She also pointed out that since this may be our last week of freedom there was nothing wrong with living it up a little. Postponing the celebration of life is a flawed human strategy, and makes as much sense as waiting to eat a meal until you see it start to rot. Thelma kept making sense under stressful conditions, and having her in my life was cause enough to celebrate every minute of every day. Africa gave us a chance to begin to catch up on our love, but everything was happening so fast. Rhoda stopped by our room to request our help with something she wanted to organize.

76

After one sip, Snopes insisted he was not a coconut mojito man, and while the two of us sat at the Komi Bar, a popular D.C. hangout, waiting for a couple of book publishers Thelma insisted it was imperative we meet, he ordered his favorite Modelo Light. He couldn't imagine who could be so important that we had to visit an exclusive haberdashery, and spend what he considered an astronomical amount on our dapper evening attire. I acted curious as well, though I knew more about the rendezvous than he did. Two beers in, Snopes damned the mystery men for not showing up on time and ranted about how success was all about precision. Halfway through beer three, he lectured that being punctilious was the edge between a great FBI agent and someone destined for demotion. I said if he keeps using words like punctilious I would have to cut the Modelos, and then ordered some appetizers. Turned out Snopes was right about timing because while he was in the restroom, our awaited duo showed up. However elegant we appeared, their sense of style was way slicker. I winked to the bartender to deliver them a pair of coconut mojitos. When Snopes returned and saw the three of us standing there, his investigative mind began sizing up the scenario. Before he could come to a complete conclusion, Rhoda, Thelma, and I raised our glasses and yelled out, "Surprise!"

As Snopes stood there stunned, Rhoda gamboled over, placed her arms around his waist, and said,

"Happy 60th handsome."

The waiter apologized that due to the busy night there was a high demand for tables of four, and asked if we minded sitting at a six top. I said we planned on ordering everything on the menu so the extra room would be welcome. As we were being seated Snopes' eyes opened wide once more when he spied two more surprises entering the eatery. Ella and Angela, carrying elaborately wrapped gifts were the reason the complicit waiter seated us this way. Snopes rose to his feet and welcomed them with loving overwhelm. That was more than enough reward to Rhoda for planning the momentous night. Beyond just a birthday party, it was a chance for us to honor someone who had his heart in the right place. Snopes had stayed one step ahead of Frumpf in keeping Thelma and me safe, as well as rich. He cared about the world and the mechanisms of a compassionate style of democracy. He didn't understand how people could protest corporate rule with a Starbucks in one hand and an Iphone in the other. He'd spent too many years alone mourning his wife and trying to erase the elements of his career that forced him to adhere to a code invented by entitled, manipulative men. Too often "in the name of national security" was uttered when the directive was a greater threat to civil liberties than the forewarned menace itself. Fellow agents would brag about how they would dodge accusations of an actual domestic dalliance by telling their spouse they couldn't account for their whereabouts "in the name of national security." Snopes despised Frumpf's administration for abusing the veil of secrecy that the concept of national security allows by refusing to make normally transparent details available to the public. White House visitor logs, business dealings, diplomatic meetings, were all now off the books, creating major distrust among the citizens. I wondered if Snopes didn't have his own hidden agenda regarding our current pilgrimage plan, as I know he would love to take Frumpf down.

Everyone's new clothes, the amazing dinner, the fine bottles of champagne, Ella and Angela's first class flight and lodging, the awaiting limo that took us all to the Smithsonian for an exclusive nighttime tour of their heirloom gardens, and the group gift to Snopes of a brand new BMW i3 electric SUV with range extender for his new life in Toronto, the evening cost over $60,000; dresser change due to the ongoing book sales of Anatomix. Still, it didn't add up to the riches Snopes felt he now possessed when at the end of the evening a gorgeously attired Rhoda danced him back to their room, claiming she had been waiting all night to go on a penis pilgrimage all their own.

Turned out to be a popular night for grand celebrations as the staff of Flimsy Fork toasted the extremely successful infomercial launch with a company dinner at New York landmark *Tavern on the Green*. Norman looked sharp in his special grey suit he usually only wore to weddings and bar mitzvahs. Though tonight he exhibited a hint of chic wearing the silk abstract tie Pauline painted herself. Maybe the success of Flimsy Fork accelerated Pauline's recent voyage from the guestroom to Thelma's former side of the bed, but their union was inevitable. As much as one can be influenced by their environment, Pauline's aesthetic remodel of Norman's home augmented his interest in the arts. He was already the company's graphic artist, but his approach was more mechanical than creative. He now enjoyed weekend gallery hopping with Pauline, discussing the creations over lunch in the village cafes. She even enticed him to don a red beret that livened his facial features with an air of avant-garde. As much as he missed Thelma, Norman's new life contained abundance in every category, and he was happy.

One person found no reason to celebrate that night. Valina's pharmaceutically based suicide was a shock to the nation. Her reputation as a spoiled socialite morphed into that of a pitied victim of political privilege overnight. Frumpf's grief was the first time his emotions bypassed his ego and went straight to his impaired heart. It was a death prayer gone badly as many citizens daily petitioned God to end Frumpf's life. Frumpf was inconsolable, and after blaming himself in every way imaginable, he then engaged his usual course of action and created a scapegoat.

Idsel was also in deep mourning as Valina was as much a daughter to him as her own father. He hoped Frumpf was summoning him for moral support, but knowing the president all too well he entertained the possibility Frumpf would skew the guilt.   Frumpf planned to site Idsel's act of malpractice in breaking Valina's confidence as the direct cause of her deep emotional demise, but when Idsel arrived at the Oval Office and looked into Frumpf's eyes, they both broke down in grief, and spent the next hour singing Valina's praises over a rare bottle of scotch gifted to Frumpf by the First Minister of Scotland. Teresa Frumpf was also devastated, as her stepdaughter had spent a ton of quality time with her over the years. Valina's death could not come at a worse time for Teresa who was about to make her divorce plans public. Announcing it now would make her seem cold and heartless.

*77

After a couple of days of mourning, Frumpf began to worry about how he would be perceived by going on a penis pilgrimage in the face of such a personal tragedy. He couldn't very well say Valina would have wanted him to get his dick back, especially in light of the past allegations of his improper behavior towards her. Snopes and I had already discussed this dilemma and turned the logistics inside out. When Frumpf's aid came to pick us up for a meeting, he claimed the president only wanted to see me, which sent my mind racing. Snopes assured me I could handle it and said if the going gets too tough to call him. Expecting to be driven to the White House I was surprised when the aid said Frumpf would be meeting me at another location.

A sutra is an aphorism in Sanskrit literature. They are texts of the oral teachings of Buddha, or in simplified terms are considered "good news." The Washington D.C. Buddhist Cultural Center had the visual pretense of a spiritual embassy and was thought of as the house of good news. I was escorted into what appeared to be a combination temple/theater where Frumpf was waiting, standing behind a podium. He waved off his aid to leave us alone, tapped on the microphone to make sure it was on, and began to speak,

"Can you hear me okay?"

I thought the question ridiculous since I was in the front row and could hear him without the microphone. He didn't wait for my reply and continued,

"As you know, I lost my daughter, and no matter who I talk to right now I feel like I'm giving a eulogy. It's easier for me to express myself when I'm on a stage than sitting quietly face-to-face. Outside of Valina, the most important person in my life is you. Pretty wild when you realize I know very little about you. Yeah, I had my people dig up your past, the little there is; home-schooling doesn't leave much of a paper trail. I had hoped we would be able to find some link to your magic, but even our intel regarding your Shaman mother gave us nothing. Too many pieces have been set in motion regarding our so-called penis pilgrimage to call if off, and the only way to get out of it is if I regain my privates beforehand. In a few minutes, we will be joined by someone who I am hoping will be able to help you to get your spiritual mumbo jumbo together, and put my problem to rest."

I tried to imagine whom he was referring to, but the only Buddhist that would even come close to that description was the Dalai Lama. No sooner had I thought it than humanity's main monk slowly made his way down the aisle towards us. The fact the president could acquire the presence of the most revered spiritual leader on earth was not what hit me, it was that Frumpf had the gall to enlist the Dalai Lama — whose global agenda of peace is compromised by almost everything the president's administration does — to help Frumpf with his penis problem.

I couldn't fathom that I was supposed to team up with him for this, or any other purpose for that matter. Does he even know why he was summoned? And how does Frumpf see this procedure playing out? Dalai and I join hands and become the men of La *Mantra*? Outside of the penis river waterfall, I have no game plan. And honestly, I can't imagine anything more humiliating than meeting this world-renowned monk as Baba Dickster. I have no lineage; I am not the 13th Dickster. I'm not ordained. His mind is calm; mine is racing faster than a lotus flower in a wind tunnel.

As the eighty-one-year-old monk reached the front of the room, I hoped to achieve immediate reincarnation. Bring me back as anything but a self-proclaimed penis swami. He was at home with who he was, unlike me who is so aware of my masquerade I feel like I'm in spiritual drag. I'm not even sure about what Frumpf has told him about me. For all I know he claimed I was a crotch magician. As the Dalai Lama approached me, I greeted him with a bow and insisted it was a great honor. He smiled and looked toward Frumpf, who was still at the podium about to speak into the mic,

"You guys need to spend some time plotting. I need to go empty my catheter."

That we both found Frumpf's statement funny instead of sad relieved some of my angst. Frumpf walked up the aisle and left. He didn't even greet or acknowledge the Dalai Lama. How freaking arrogant is that? Maybe the president sees the Dalai Lama as some kind of trendy warlock. As he sat next to me in the front row, his words were surreal,

"I enjoyed your book. Although I have no ability to cause miracles, I am happy to be in the presence of such a master."

This can't be happening, I thought.

"I'm no miracle worker. I'm not even a real guru. I'm just a guy with a weird gift no one understands, not even me. You really liked my book," I replied.

The Dalai Lama said, "I am also just a guy many don't understand."

We spent the next half hour discussing my power over genitalia, and the Dalai Lama claimed he could have used me when he was negotiating peace with the Chinese leaders in Tibet. I asked if he would have threatened them with castration, and he said "threat" was not in his vocabulary but there is nothing wrong with firm, peaceful negotiation. He was very funny and awkwardly normal. He informed me that he already had this dilemma all figured out, and would reveal it to Frumpf. I now knew why people kiss his feet; he is so damn useful. When Frumpf re-entered, the Dalai Lama motioned with his hands for him to sit next to me. He then approached the podium, tapped the mic to see if it was on, and turned it off.

"Sometimes, not getting what you want, when you want it, is a stroke of good luck," he said.

Frumpf and I sat waiting for him to continue, but that was it. There was no intricate plan, no promise of a special blessing, and no road to penile enlightenment, just a simple affirmation, and Frumpf seemed far from affirmed. I did think it was cool though, how he turned off the sound before he spoke.

Fortunately for the president, what the Dalai Lama lacked in creative planning, Snopes possessed in spades. Snopes' idea was to spread Valina's ashes at Lourdes, an integral stop on the pilgrimage, claiming it was one of Valina's favorite places in the world. Had it been anyone but Frumpf he would never have suggested such a sham, but the president was a fabulist, and Snopes believed he would say anything if it meant getting his dick back.

147

Former model slash actress slash singer Cheryl Miles was Valina's birth mama. Being the president's ex-wife wasn't a perk fest; except for the hush money they paid her to keep stories of Frumpf's previous sexual escapades silent during the campaign. Not that odysseys of the flesh like a ménage a trois, bisexual liaison, or Dominican Republic orgy were consequential to the voting public when his pussy grabbing boasts mattered not. When Cheryl heard the news of Frumpf's plan to spread Valina's ashes at the Catholic pilgrimage site she went ballistic. Cheryl not only knew Frumpf's claim of Valina's love for Lourdes was fiction, but she was also aware her daughter hated Catholicism because it gave priests a perverted platform to molest young boys. Cheryl called Frumpf, warning he will burn in hell, and threatened to post her complete collection of compromising photos all over the web. How sick is it that Frumpf's first thought was people would at least see him with a dick again? Still, he was well aware of Cheryl's racy pics, and right now his crotch was already enough of a superstar. Frumpf notified us about the mama threat at noon, but by five p.m. Cheryl called him back having reconsidered, declaring she thinks of Valina as her little miracle, so the waters of the grotto were the ideal spot to spread her spirit. Frumpf called thinking he was giving us a heads up, unaware that we already knew, and had used the persuasive power people possess when they have access to millions of dollars of book royalties.

To regain the massive energy spent on our *'we may lose our freedom in a few days sexual mania'*, Thelma and I lunched on room service fare. I found it quite eccentric that my meeting with the Tibetan monk made her horny, and even more outlandish was her claim that her vagina now had only one degree of separation from the Dalai Lama. I began to visualize how that math might work, but immediately concluded I didn't want to know. She inquired if we exchanged emails and if I had invited him to come on the pilgrimage. I voiced it was my hope never to bring up the word penis in his presence again. There was something the Dalai Lama offered to help me with, but until I knew more, I decided not to share. When I told her he complimented my book she thought I was joking, but when I insisted he said he loved it, she flipped, and immediately called Ella and Angela who helped us put *Anatomix* together.

The night before the commencement of the Presidential Penis Pilgrimage was daunting. I felt like I was Jeff Sessions about to play one-on-one with LeBron James. Even when Snopes claimed we would have the whole Air Force-1 first class press cabin to ourselves, all I could think of was tomorrow morning I had to become *Penis Guru Baba Dickster*, remaining in character in front of the whole world for days, not to mention the pressure of accomplishing a mystical, presidential penile regeneration I have no ability to perform. Thelma said all I could do was give it my best shot, to which I replied if I failed they're going to line us up against a wall and give us theirs. We were about to accompany the president on a jet that is armored to withstand a nuclear explosion, thwart missiles by dazzling infrared guidance systems, but had no onboard feature to protect us from the tribulations of traveling with Frumpf. Thelma and I have enough money right now to vanish, and never be seen again. She kept saying she had faith in me, but if I really wanted to run she would follow me to the ends of the earth. What I needed was a sign.

The universe works in wild ways, and when I went to the lobby to meet with whom it delivered I was shocked at the physical transformation of Norman, Norman, Norman. His posture had acquired the spine of confidence, and his red beret confirmed there were a canvass, brush, and palette nearby. When he saw me approaching, his demeanor was much more welcoming than I deserved. We sat on a nearby lobby sofa.

"So this is quite a surprise," I said.

Norman smiled, and admitted,

"You changed my life, Sheldon. Everything that has occurred since Thelma left me has been amazing. Pauline is an incredible influence, and together we've delved into studying art history. The past has no better means of preservation than what is recorded through the eyes and hands of the artist, and as we inspect their archival transcriptions it is beyond obvious they have witnessed miracles. You are about to embark on a journey whose story will be interpreted and chronicled by every medium that exists. Paintings, sculptures, songs, poems, will all depict the tale of the miracle you are about to perform."

"Wow Norman, quite the soliloquy, but as I keep reminding everyone, I don't perform miracles." I said.

Norman took my right hand firmly in his, and said,

"If you spent one minute in my new life, or Pauline or Thelma's heart, you would know you already have performed miracles. Maybe you'll give the president what he hopes for, maybe not, but I guarantee when this is over you will have transformed enough of the world to make your supernatural prowess impossible to deny."

He handed me a nicely wrapped small box and said,

"This is for Frumpf. Have an amazing trip."

It was hard to believe Norman would travel from New York to D.C. just to set me straight, so I imagined whatever was in the box must have been extremely important. When I told Thelma Norman was here and gone she was shocked, and I could tell a bit disappointed he didn't want to at least say hello to her. She shook the box a bit, looked at it from different angles, and placed it on the table.

"Should we open it?" I asked.

Thelma shared my curiosity, as anyone who had been handed a mystery box to give to the president would.

"He said it was for Frumpf," she declared.

Although I wanted to rip off that wrapping paper so fast and rationalized we should make sure it was safe, it was not my box. I had already defied Norman once by unwrapping the greatest gift, Thelma, so I accepted its mystery. As it sat on the table, it became such a curious thing we nicknamed it Pandora's box. Somehow Norman had done it. Not only had he influenced me to believe that my power may prove miraculous, but also his box distracted me from my worries enough to consider sleep.

With eyes closed, I wondered about how evil the president really was. Narcissism, his most rancid trait is certainly morally foul and devoid of compassion, but when someone possesses a personality disorder does that make them sinister, or merely broken? Does evil require one to be conscious of what drives their ugly behavior, and where do we draw the line between mentally handicapped and calculatingly cruel? Would seeing Frumpf as a victim of brain damage, as opposed to a manipulative master of corruption, alleviate a portion of the spell, and begin to repair his groin before we get to Penis River? When we faced the Zambian lion, Thelma's oration to incite me to believe the lion was evil instead of hungry may have inspired my power. Maybe it was possible to undo Frumpf's dicklessness by adjusting my view of his character, or lack of, as opposed to the impossible task of inducing him to improve it himself.

80

Frumpf was addicted to insisting. Now instead of taking the helicopter to the tarmac where Air Force One awaited our arrival, he insisted we take the motorcade, so the public had the chance to line the streets and cheer the Penis Pilgrimage's success. It was obvious to me that the word penis suited the president's lips way more than that of the Dalai Lama. Frumpf gave into his addiction once again by *insisting* only I travel in his car, leaving the rest of the gang to follow along in the shiny black herd of his cavalcade. So onward we trudged on this auspicious Monday morning. Snopes, Rhoda, Thelma, Frumpf, Dickster, and a myriad of Secret Service, ventured out on the first leg of a journey I wished was over before it started.

From my vantage point in the first lady's seat, Frumpf seemed inordinately happy for a man who was going through the things he described to Snopes and me during his office rant. He acted like instead of taking a dismal journey that would culminate in the most publicized failure in history; we were on our way to pick up his lost dick. His optimism was equal parts enviable and annoying. He suggested we wait to bring back what he was now calling his "pretty package" until the finale at Penis River. Frumpf imagined the suspense would create an enormous amount of attention, which would translate into inflated support for a successful outcome. I reminded him that the actual result might not show up for as along as a month, but he pushed that climax aside insisting he could sense my power will do him right. Did he stay up all night reading Eckhart Tolle? Did his momentary brush with Buddhism the other day seep into his soul? Even the fact that the support he imagined would line the streets was sparse, consisting of protest signs claiming he was a dick and hoped he disappeared; nothing constrained his optimistic frame of mind.

Thinking he was turning over a new leaf was short lived as he shared a plan he had devised to stick it to Queen Elizabeth for refusing to host him during our visit. His greatest disappointment wasn't even not being invited to Buckingham Palace, which he described as a "sad, musty, archaic bunch of oversized stones," but that he wasn't going to get to ride in the lavish, gold-plated Diamond Jubilee State Coach, which other foreign dignitaries, including Chinese President Xi Jinping, and Mexican President Enrique Peña Nieto used during past state visits. When Frumpf shared he arranged being greeting at the UK tarmac by a crowned, famous drag queen, I laughed but hoped he was kidding.

It was comforting to be reunited with my cohorts in our deluxe cabin at the rear of Air Force One. After take-off we played with all the high tech communication gadgets and discussed what we wanted to do when the pilgrimage was over. Thelma suggested she and I start an immigration housing organization for displaced Syrian refugees and their animals that survived being left behind. Rhoda and Snopes didn't have a pet project in mind but were very supportive of Thelma's idea. Snopes' present dream was more family oriented, and he wanted to figure out something that would keep Ella and Angela close by. In my best Baba Dickster voice, I said I would be happy as long as the Penis River didn't turn around and fuck me in the ass. No sooner had I said "ass," than Frumpf himself stopped by our cabin. He claimed that reports from the ground confirmed that there were thousands awaiting out flight, and although there were many protestors, the majority were there to welcome Baba Dickster. He said the executive menu was available to us throughout the pilgrimage, and not to be shy about eating and drinking to our heart's content. When Rhoda said thank you, he replied,

"Don't thank me, the taxpayers are footing the bill."

Oh those taxpayers, millions of people that are unconstitutionally bullied into giving an ever rising percentage of their hard earned buck to the government so they could mostly make interest payments to the Federal Reserve who lend the regime money that doesn't really exist. Part of Frumpf's campaign platform was tax reform that would have made wealthy corporations pay their fair share, but his current policies have done the complete opposite. Even his healthcare bill aimed to un-insure millions while giving the upper one percent the kind of tax relief that made Uncle Sam seem more like a brother. To make matters worse, Frumpf's lavish lifestyle had already cost the country more in the first few weeks than the previous president's first two years.

*81

Deep within a dense forest of coniferous blue-green cedar that is considered the Himalayan Wood of the Gods rests the Dalai Lama's home in Dharamsala. Perched high atop a majestic precipice, his residence boasts a view of the valley that separates the Indian subcontinent from his long lost holy land, Tibet. Incorporating doctrinal teaching into the numbskull nexus of current society is a complex procedure that relies on support from brilliant scholars whose philosophies coincide with his strong belief in never ignoring the value of scientific research. Equally important is the effort to translate the ancient scriptures to concepts easily grasped by the mainstream. *"A barrel of laughs will bring more peace than the barrel of a gun,"* was a saying created by a well-respected disciple Yuva Yatree. Today Yuva's presence was requested by the Dalai Lama to discuss a special project supposedly only Yuva could assist him with. Yuva was inordinately elated and brought along his dranyen; a six string instrument similar to the guitar, in hope he might get the chance to play the Dalai Lama a song he had written about him.

82

Aussie Comedian, Larry Hampton, was known throughout the world for his portrayal as Dame Ethel; a female character whose lighthearted lampooning of London's nobility allowed her to live the very fame she satirized. Although Hampton had retired the previous year after a long and successful career, there she was, adorned in a crown to mockingly welcome Frumpf to England. The public perceived it as a jab to her majesty; they considered it disgraceful and labeled Frumpf a "Royal Asshole." His motivation was childishly vindictive, but I am not sure it was any more contemptuous than what the Royal Family inflicts on the UK itself. Here's a country full of sophisticated artists, intellects, and innovators. They gave us the Beatles and Rolling Stones for fuck's sake! A nation with a rich history of statespersons such as Churchill and Albright, and what are they mostly known for? Palaces, princesses, and the scuttlebutt of pomp. Their closed system of class society erases any hope for a commoner to rise through the royal ranks, which is where Frumpf leaves them in the dust as he has shown that no matter how unqualified, unintelligent, or radically ill-mannered someone may be, they can still ascend to the position of the president of the United States of America.

Stonehenge was not the same when surrounded by hundreds of spectators there to observe the first leg of Baba Dickster's wizardry. Enthusiasts held up and wore all kinds of phallic creations. Entrepreneurial vendors hawked "Presidential Penis Pilgrimage" T-shirts, hats, and banners. The area directly around the monument itself was roped off for just Dickster and Frumpf. The photos clicked, the video cameras rolled, and the silence I had hoped for to create the ambiance of a sacred process disintegrated from shape. As I peered across the ropes at Thelma, she smiled her complicity. I positioned Frumpf to sit facing the semicircle stone configuration I sat towards on my last journey. To the suspenseful crowd, it was uneventful until a cluster of ominous clouds gathered directly above us, and began spiraling downward in an uncommonly rapid pace. Frumpf looked at me for reassurance that we weren't about to be abducted to Mars, and though, his guess was as good as mine, I nodded with confidence that it was part of the pilgrimage process. When the bystanders witnessed that it began to rain on only the two of us, their murmuring became deafening. Out of the corner of my eye, I saw Snopes nodding his head in appreciation of nature's theatrics. Frumpf suddenly experienced a pang in his crotch and instinctively touched it to check if some kind of growth was taking place. Not since Janet Jackson's Super Bowl nipple peek has such attention been paid to one person's private area. The crowd's attention was so blatant that when his touch revealed no new appendage, he shook his head 'no' to let everyone know the magic moment had not yet occurred.

I found relief in the safety of our private Air Force One cabin that thwarted the press, who were hounding me to reveal the significance of the inexplicable two-man rainstorm that simulating baptism by the heavens. In my best Swami-speak possible I told them they would have to witness more pieces of the puzzle to see the full picture. Snopes slapped me on the back assuring me I gave an Oscar winning performance, but he also wondered about the significance of the cloud conjuring event. I shrugged and wrote it off as a possible byproduct of mass condensation caused by the heat of the crowd that had been centrally magnetized to the opposing cooling of the massive stone pillars. I quickly added,

"I truthfully had no fucking clue."

Since our next stop was France, which by direct flight was only an hour away, Frumpf determined we wouldn't fly again until morning. Because anything I did the next day would be overshadowed by Frumpf's cremation ceremony to spread Valina's ashes at the healing grotto, I felt relaxed and suggested we do some of that eating and drinking Frumpf offered. Frumpf soon showed up at our cabin and invited us to dine with him at six o'clock. None of us were really interested in hanging out with him anymore than necessary, but as Rhoda so humanely pointed out; if we couldn't have compassion for someone that is without his wife, without his dick, and about to honor his deceased daughter, who he had loved maybe more that he should have, then how did we ever expect to bridge what she called the world's divide. So as an act of selfless diplomacy, we all agreed to dine with someone that made us sick.

*83

When Yuva Yatree departed from his meeting with the Dalai Lama, it was difficult to discern whether his demeanor represented deep thought or sadness. There was no doubt his time with the Buddhist master was highly coveted, and the Dalai Lama even seemed thoroughly touched by Yuva's song. The problem was the venture the Dalai Lama presented was life changing. Turning down the request of the Dalai Lama was not something a follower would even consider, as it was seen as the ultimate privilege to serve him. But Yuva was told to meditate about his potential participation and was promised that whatever he decided would be accepted with the utmost respect.

84

It takes only one dinner with the president to understand why his potbelly looked like he too suffered from the demise of Planned Parenthood. After a couple of cocktails it was overly tempting to pat him on the stomach while expressing concern about the fate of the polar bear. We all refrained. Frumpf clearly ate for comfort more than nutrition, <u>his</u> comfort because there was nothing comfortable about watching him eat. He was the ultimate omnivore, yet not concerned at all about the thousands of people in his own country who were eating nothing at all. In this way, he was a classic conservative Republican. They hemmed and hawed about the depravity of abortion, but once the child was born, they could care less if the kid starved to death.

After what was admittedly one of the best pieces of chocolate cake any of us had ever had, Thelma stood up and said in appreciation for his "fusalodging" she would like to present him with a little token and handed Frumpf the nicely wrapped box Norman had given me for him. Frumpf looked genuinely touched, joking he would have to take it to the security room first to have it X-rayed. He asked if he should open it now and joked again by asking if it was his new penis. We all found that funny. When he opened it up, it looked like some kind of commercial product. As he read the label, he asked,

"What the hell is a Flimsy Fork?"

The winged White House took off at seven a.m. through a UK rainstorm we quipped was the Queen's response to Frumpf's impertinence yesterday. Not that it mattered, as this plane was built to fly through a hurricane of missiles. Thelma was worried Norman's gift might have been seen as poor taste, and it was possible Frumpf took it like we were making fun of his rotundity. She decided to apologize, and when she arrived at the dining room, Frumpf was sitting there eating a large breakfast using the Flimsy Fork. He lit up when he saw her, and declared,

"I love this thing, best gift ever."

Thelma thought if Norman could only witness this scene.

"I've haven't tried it yet," Thelma said.

Frumpf pulled out a chair and motioned for Thelma to sit with him. Using his finger, he motioned for his aid to bring Thelma all the breakfast accoutrements.

"Where did you get this thing," The president asked.

"My husband works for the company that invented it. He would be thrilled to see you using it," Thelma said.

The president turned his body towards her and struck a pose of him taking a bite of his food using the fork. He nodded to his aid, who was apparently accustomed to Frumpf's silent commands, and smiled as the aid took a photo of him using the odd utensil. He turned to Thelma and said,

"I'll have it emailed it to Dickster."

Although the photo was a nice gesture, it was also Frumpf's way of fucking with her by sending a photo of her husband's product to her boyfriend. It was as if Frumpf had a special talent to add confrontation to anything he did.

Frumpf continued, "We've come a long way you and I. You were there during the assassination attempt, instrumental at my gala castration, and now the amazing Penis Pilgrimage. When this is all over, and I am what the vice president calls "retooled," maybe you would be interested in joining me for some executive privilege."

As an aid placed a fancy array of breakfast food in front of her, Thelma wanted immediately to excuse herself from Frumpf's presence. She was astounded that even penisless he was propositioning her. She pitied all the women who accused him of harassment during his campaign that he publically condemned as lying opportunists seeking fame and fortune. She realized even the Flimsy Fork photo gesture might have been part of his manipulative vaginal courtship. She took a few nibbles of her eggs as not to be equally rude, and as she got up from her chair to leave, she said,

"Mr. President, although I appreciate your interest in my personal platform, in regards to your proposal I am way less liberal than you think."

She then spilled her coffee on his white shag rug and left.

Back in the rear cabin Thelma sat with me while Snopes and Rhoda were showering, getting ready for the day.

"You actually referred to your vagina as your personal platform," I asked.

Thelma said it was a bit of a misrepresentation, and with a naughty tone claimed it was now *my* personal platform. She wondered if Frumpf's inappropriate proposal was really about sex or his constant need for validation. It wasn't as if the president and I were buds now, but we did have what one might call a working relationship, and I have to admit that his attempt to arrange a tryst with Thelma using a dick I was in the process of regenerating was not only uninspiring but also self-sabotaging on his part, to say the least.

*85

The French dialect has a reputation for being the language of love. The flowing balance between consonants and vowels help their phrases float off the tongue. Genitalia, a word that is already one of the subtlest dick references in the English language, takes on an even more romantic timbre when the French call it "organes génitaux." Unfortunately today the French people of the Pyrenees will repeat a word in protest that has never rolled off of anyone's tongue, 'Frumpf.' The president could care less about their vocal opposition and told us that the French are totally ungrateful. His fractured reasoning was that we gave them Jerry Lewis, and all we got was some androgynous green statue.   As he said that, I realized that Frumpf doesn't see the spirit or meaning in anything, continually judging everything by outward appearances. What was meant to give Lady Liberty the image of strength to eternally hold up the guiding torch of prosperity, Frumpf saw as masculinity, and even claimed she might be a "tranny."

The five-mile hike to Lourdes to capture some of the elements of being on an actual pilgrimage was whittled down by Frumpf to a ten-minute stroll, which was still more exercise than he has had in weeks since he tweaked his lower back trying to swat a passing sparrow on the greens with his 5 iron. His greatest concern right now had nothing to do with his dick for a change and was more about spreading Valina's ashes. First, he complained the box the ashes were in was wrong, and it should have been a golden urn. He claimed he should have never taken Snopes' advice to pretend this was something Valina would have appreciated. He then decided he would not go ahead with the Valina sham, and instructed his aids to find his ex-wife Cheryl who was waiting at the site and escort her back to the States.   In a matter of minutes, Frumpf restructured all of his focus on getting his dick back. He then asked me what the fuck it meant that this place was famous for a *Marian apparition*.

I had enough on my mind without worrying about Frumpf's constant amendments to our planned pilgrimage procedure. Snopes on the other hand commended the president for his modification, and said the Valina ceremony would have been an unnecessary distraction. He went on to say sometimes it's important to alter a plan to achieve one's ultimate goal. Frumpf was in complete agreement, but something about Snopes' tone when he made that statement made me think he was planning on doing some alterations of his own.

Most of the boycotting along the road to the sacred grotto consisted of protest signs and voiced disparaging slogans. The fact it was all in French made it less demeaning because Frumpf didn't understand any of it, allowing his arrogant mind to perceive it as support for his plight, a concept he would even portray to the media. He was always on the lookout for a way to make disapproval appear otherwise, which is why when we arrived at the Grotto of Massabielle, in the Sanctuary of Our Lady of Lourdes, where the Virgin Mary had given instructions to drink and bathe in the holy spring, his spinning ability came to a halt.

Thirty full-time chaplains under the tutelage of the Roman Catholic Bishop of Tarbes oversee the domain of Lourdes where almost seventy miracles have supposedly transpired over the years. Every one of the chaps was now lined up in front of the spring preventing us from entering. The head chaplain apologized, but claimed due to an edict presented by the Vatican it was determined it would be sacrilegious to allow the use of the spring to recover someone's "organes génitaux." This time the phrase didn't roll off the tongue. He expanded the decree to say even though the president's reputation for trying to undo the separation of church and state was appreciated by the diocese, and his recent appointment of a Supreme Court judge who was against abortion was admirable, they were afraid the publicity of a penis miracle would attract the wrong kind of pilgrim. He then handed the president an envelope and asked us to retreat from the premises.

"Alone at midnight," Frumpf exclaimed as he read the Chaplain's note to us back on the plane.

"I'm not meeting with a bunch of sexually repressed robed deviants in a grotto in the middle of the night. What do they think this is, the Playboy Mansion? How are we supposed to keep the hype happening if we have to keep the miracle under wraps?" He ranted.

He immediately insisted that I come with him, and had his chauffeur bring us back to the Grotto. He instructed the driver to pull right up to the foot of the steps. He jumped out of the car with me in tow and claimed this is how a real pilgrim gets things done. With only two chaplains at the spring now and a handful on their way up the stairway in pursuit, Frumpf charged the Sacred

Grotto and plunged in fully clothed. As I stood at the edge with the astounded coterie of the Catholic brigade, I watched as Frumpf splashed the water all over himself, making sure it went down the front of his pants.

"Hey, I thought you guys liked resurrections," he mocked.

At which time the president of these United States of America, a man who is supposed to garner global respect, cupped his hands like a drinking vessel, scooped up a serving of holy water, brought it to his mouth, and began gargling so loud it even drowned out the chaplain's group gasp.

It was no surprise when French President Francois Hollande canceled Frumpf's dinner invitation. There was no mention of the grotto transgression, and in the name of diplomacy Hollande apologized, claiming he had a sudden family emergency he had to attend to. Frumpf acknowledged he had no remorse for his "spring fling." He said their dopey Disneyland would be lucky to have the reputation of resurrecting a schlong such as his. He claimed if the Virgin Mary were there to witness the reappearance of his dick she would be so tempted by its beauty her actions would disqualify her from ever using the word Virgin in her name again.

Was it a disregard for religion, or an innate disrespect for women that would allow him to depict the mother of Jesus as someone who couldn't resist fucking him? Frumpf said religion was merely another vote generator, and though his comments may seem crude and sacrilegious, there wasn't a member of his party that gave a rat's ass whether or not Mary's story was covering up a sweaty night with a broken condom. I told him they didn't have condoms back then, to which he replied,

"Well they had dicks, so let's keep our eyes on the ball."

When the press released photos of Frumpf pulling out the front of his trousers to allow the Grotto's holy water to bathe his *Executive Zone*, the president was beside himself with satisfaction. If one can ascend their position of stature based on telephoto images, Frumpf's chauffeur would now be secretary of state. No longer that farfetched a concept since almost everyone in Frumpf's cabinet was given their post based on favors rather than qualifications. I wondered if the diocese would be more upset about the off color publicity, or the fact their healing springs, in this case, would be seen as effective as Evian.

As all of us now perceived Air Force One as a hideout from potential religious retribution, we were relieved when Frumpf ordered the plane to depart France, and begin our thirteen-hour flight to the more spiritually merciful land of Cambodia. While I sat at the window watching a lightening storm illuminate the clouds, Snopes joined me, and said he needed to discuss a little idea he had. It was now his opinion that giving Frumpf back his dick was the wrong thing to do. He was sure that making it vanish wasn't my doing, and I was merely the tool of fate. He believed that comparative suffering was the only thing that could ever cause a man like Frumpf to finally have compassion for the rest of the world, but if we could end his presidency than it wouldn't matter. I asked him if he was suggesting we make him choose one or the other, dick or dictatorship? Before he could answer, I said he would never go for it, and even if he did, how could we guarantee he would follow through? Snopes insisted we wouldn't have to, and all we needed to do is refuse to complete the pilgrimage until Frumpf releases his tax returns.

Frumpf's tax returns were probably the biggest bone of contention in the USA. More than half the country was marching in demand that he release them, and his reluctance led most to believe the contents held secrets that would disqualify him from holding office. I asked Snopes when he came up with this idea, and he claimed it had been brewing for quite a while, but he was reluctant to share it with me earlier as it might have affected my healing of Frumpf. He said it was Thelma's story regarding Frumpf's inappropriate incursion that finally sealed the deal.

When I told Thelma what Snopes suggested she was concerned his reaction could be explosive, and that we needed to think the whole thing through. If he believed Penis River would bring his dick back he would have no choice but to agree to our terms, but if he thought the chances were slim he could turn us down and then *trump up* charges of treason, and who knows what else. She suggested we wait as long as we could to spring this on him, surmising the closer he got to being potentially reunited with his dick, the more likely he would agree to our request.

86

Circling Siem Reap on our approach to land allowed me to try and spot the Penis River from above. I had a vague map in my head of where it was in relation to the pervasive Angkor Wat main temple. I felt a profound connection when I spied it peak through the jungle canopy. The ensuing performance of a miracle I had been preoccupied with the last few days has now been replaced by imagining Frumpf's face when we dish out our tax return ultimatum. I was sure Snopes was right that the ultimate irony is giving Frumpf back his dick in exchange for *unfucking* America.

The crowd at the Siem Reap tarmac was nothing like their European counterparts. There were no protest signs, no angry cries, just a large group of Cambodians waiting to see the dickless man the rest of the world was talking about. Baba Dickster was barely on their radar, and it was now all about Frumpf. As the press filmed the president mingling with a happy looking crowd, I could almost hear the gears of propaganda turning in Frumpf's mind. "Asia love Frumpf," was the headline he imagined. "Cambodia welcomes greatest global peacemaker," he thought. "Racist reluctantly shakes hands with natives for the sake of promotion," I pictured.

Frumpf was anxious to get the show on the road and insisted we head out to Penis River immediately to attend to his crotch reunion. I hadn't finalized the plan with Snopes regarding the timing of our insubordination. We were then informed an animal had set off a random land mine, the explosion of which caused part of the road to the river to be under repair, which made our only immediate route to our destination a one-hour trek through the jungle. I was glad they said animal, and avoided the beast's description in detail, as it made me feel less guilty about the fact the news of postponement was a relief.

Frumpf had all kinds of questions. Were there snakes? Was there a chance we could encounter a land mine? When would the road be fixed? When the Cambodian guide said it could be a few days, and the jungle trek would be safe, the president decided we should immediately head out. Rhoda, Snopes, Thelma, five reporters, four Secret Service, the guide, and me as Baba Dickster, did not give off the presence of a pilgrimage, but instead a parade. What was supposed to take an hour wound up being two because Frumpf required a rest every ten minutes. When we finally arrived at the Stung Kbal Spean river site, Frumpf's exhaustion turned to excitement. As he spied some of the carved phallic shapes in the riverbed, it made him feel like his penile purgatory was almost over. He turned towards the reporters, whose cameras were capturing the surroundings, and began to give a speech,

"You are all about to experience the reward of believing in the human spirit. This pilgrimage was not just about anatomy but proving what we are capable of when we have faith. Why don't you say a few words Baba Dickster?"

As the cameras turned towards me, I looked over at Snopes who gave me a thumbs-up. I hadn't planned on including the press in our mutiny, but sticking it to him on tape seemed par for the course. I channeled my most sincere Baba Dickster personae, and spoke into the camera,

"There is no greater miracle in this world than love."

I looked over at Thelma who winked at me. I continued,

"In the last few days of traveling with the president I've gained a clear perspective of his worldview and beliefs. I now know how he truly feels about religion, human rights, and even romance."

One of the reporters asked, "What does he think about romance?"

I thanked the reporter for her question, and said,

"The only sign of love I have heard him express is the love for himself. It is with this knowledge that I have decided that the only way I can restore his genitalia is if he agrees to release his tax returns right now."

The press immediately turned the cameras toward Frumpf, who insisted they shut them off as he addressed me directly,

"Listen to me you whiny wizard, you will complete this pilgrimage right now, or I will have the whole lot of you jailed for insubordination."

If you've never spent an hour in the jungle listening to a world leader's threats, you ought to try it sometime as it is not only amusing, but you get to experience how their mind works under pressure when another entity defies them. If I were the leader of N. Korea, he would have already bombed my hospitals, killed my family, and tortured me into compliance. I repeatedly tried to explain to Frumpf that the likelihood of successfully completing our mission under this kind of duress was highly doubtful, and if he had any hopes of even masturbating again, he needed to order the release of his tax returns immediately. As Snopes and I predicted, Frumpf agreed to release them if and when his penis regeneration was effective, which of course we knew he wouldn't do as he already reneged on his promise to the whole nation that he would release them after the election.

As time marched forward, he changed his tact, and attempted to appeal to our compassion. Now that Valina was dead he wanted to have another child, and needed his dick back, he said. Even if he agreed to release his returns it would take quite a while because they weren't yet completed, he informed us. He went on and on, but I realized if I did agree to perform the final magic, and it didn't work, he would be as angry and vindictive as ever now, so my only *trump card* was keeping the future dream alive.

Since we only planned for a three-hour jaunt, no one had food, and Frumpf was hungry. It was also getting late, and the mosquitoes had an appetite as well. To top it off, it looked like we were expecting rain. Traipsing through a muddy jungle trail during a downpour did not make Frumpf happier. By the look on his face, this was the worst day of his life. When we got back to the plane, he had nothing to say to us, and we all retreated to our respective cabins.

The mood in our cabin was dire. We had followed through with our plan, but we were now unsure of what was next. Rhoda insinuated there was no way he would give up on his dick, and after he saw I was not budging he would have no choice but to release his returns. Thelma said if this were a movie he would threaten to kill her if I didn't comply. My greatest concern was what would happen to all of us if he released his returns, and I still couldn't make his dick reappear, which was likely the case. We had just raised the stakes, and we needed a strategy. Snopes reminded us that none of this is about us. If we bring down his administration through his tax revelations, then nothing else matters. We're doing this for the planet. But were we? With Frumpf gone would everything be ok? The government was still overrun by a maniacal Republican majority in every branch, and the empty Supreme Court seat that should have been filled by the former president had now been bullishly filled through a fucked up rightwing tactic called the "nuclear option." Would the world really be saved? Doubtful. I don't even believe most of Frumpf's policies are his because after spending all this time with him it is clear he has no insight to what he is promoting and is just an arrogant, selfish, kneejerk-twittering-puppet.

87

The Flimsy Fork conference room was packed. Zoomed large on a big screen in front of the room was the photo Thelma forwarded to Norman of Frumpf using their invention. CEO Ted Landers was taking a poll to determine who thought using Frumpf's image would help sell the product or would it hurt their status. The idea Frumpf was a promotional liability was unanimous, but Norman who in the past would usually only observe said,

"What if we say Flimsy Fork can get rid of the president, only one pound at a time?"

Hearing Norman speak out was enough of a shock, but hearing something brilliant come out of him was astonishing, and the room applauded as if he announced he was engaged, which unbeknownst to anyone but he and Pauline was the case. Ted asked to see Norman in his office and left the room.

Last Sunday, while visiting a figurative abstract *art from scrap* exhibit, Pauline noticed one of the figures was wearing a beautiful white gold, sapphire ring. When she pointed it out to Norman, he encouraged her to try it on. She slapped him on the shoulder and lectured that handling art pieces was a no-no. He asked her if it was a no-no if he had the artist put it there to encourage her to say yes-yes. She asked, "Did you?"

At which point Norman removed the ring from the sculpture's finger, got on his knees and said,

"Pauline Castleman, will you be my masterpiece?"

To which she responded, "Yes, yes."

Ted Landers was not your cliché CEO type. He was not in it just for the money but actually believed Flimsy Fork would help millions of people that were suffering from obesity in the United States. It was clearly out of hand when airlines were trying to charge passengers by the pound. That America needed a weight loss solution right now that made more sense than carcinogenic sugar substitutes and liposuction.

When Norman entered Ted's office, he was asked to have a seat. Ted gave him kudos for his Frumpf campaign idea.

Norman said, "We got rid of his dick, his belly should be no problem."

Ted said that is what he wanted to talk to him about. He was curious how Norman finagled the Frumpf fork photo. The tone of Ted's inquisition felt a bit accusatory, but Norman just said his soon to be ex-wife got it for him.

"The soon to be ex-wife who is now hanging out with the Dickster crowd involved in the whole penis pilgrimage scandal," Ted said.

This was the first time Norman heard it referred to as a scandal and wondered how he knew about Thelma's affiliation. Ted turned his cell phone screen towards Norman and pressed play. It was the full press footage of my riverside Frumpf tax ultimatum showing my line about love, and Thelma winking. Still, Norman didn't see how Thelma's relationship with Dickster affected the company in any way. Ted said since Thelma was Norman's wife she legally co-owns his stake in the company, and if word gets out Dickster's gal is one of us they could be screwed. Norman claimed more than half the country is behind Dickster's demand Frumpf releases his tax returns. Ted claimed it was the wrong half, because as he put it,

"The disillusioned half follows Frumpf because they believe he's going to rescue them. Those are the same fat fucks that would buy Flimsy Fork. No one with any table manners or sophistication is going to eat with a utensil that makes the food drop back onto the plate. The Frumpf fans are who we're targeting."

Norman considered Ted's assessment, and wondered why then would using Frumpf's photo be seen as a liability.

Ted continued,

"And as far as connecting the dots go, it is now obvious to me, and hopefully not to anyone else in this company that you must have had something to do with Handy Randy's dickless day. I'm not sure why that went down, but it's way too coincidental now, which is why I am going to have to let you go."

88

The footage of my refusal to complete the penis pilgrimage kept reappearing on the evening news as they turned the situation into a "SITUATION." It was now,

DAY 2 OF STANDOFF AT PENIS RIVER.

Although we were all back on opposite ends of Air Force One, the media kept showing shots of the waterfall and surrounding stone phallic carvings along the riverbed. Local guides were cashing in charging tourists to be taken to the site.

Back in the USA, opposing protests clashed as if the future of Frumpf's dick was the most important issue on earth. Although the majority wanted Frumpf's taxes released, there were millions who cared only about getting him his dick back. Jimmy Fallon's Tonight Show even created a mock game show called,

Tax Returns or Penis Returns – you be the judge.

We were afraid to leave our Air Force One cabin since we were unsure if there were fanatical angry Frumpf fans wandering around. I was once revered as his potential healer, but now they saw me as the enemy. There was no doubt many of the most outspoken Frumpf supporters were paid by his administration to create a wave of hysteria, not unlike during his presidential campaign, but it was impossible to prove, and thanks to Frumpf's M.O. of calling anything he didn't like *Fake News,* his supporters only believe what he and Fox News tells them to. I don't think Frumpf even understood the damage to democracy he did by diminishing the country's faith in not only news reporting, but science as well. If we now deny science and call factual findings fake, we should forgive all student debt because if knowledge no longer has value how can you charge a student for showing them how to accumulate it?

On the morning of day three, a Frumpf aid informed us he would like to meet with Thelma in the dining room. She was a bit intimidated, having been hit on during her last visit, but we all encouraged her to see what he wanted and reminded her she had little concern because he was penisless. When Thelma arrived, Frumpf was leaning on the table in his robe appearing like he hadn't slept in a week. He was unshaven and disheveled. Unlike his usual breakfast feast, he was just nursing a cup of black coffee and a piece of dry toast. Thelma doubted he would let her photograph that image.

"Quite a sight, if Hillary could only see me now," Frumpf said, referring to his former election opponent.

Thelma felt empathy for his apparent depression, but because he was Frumpf, she also imagined it could easily be a manipulative ruse.

"I've seen you look better," she replied.

Thelma sat on the opposite side of the table as an aid delivered a cappuccino.

"I would say extra hot like you like it but I know you would think I meant something besides the cappuccino. That's the hole I dug, and no one believes anything I say, or they think I mean something else than what I'm trying to communicate. I'm not all bad you know. I've never admitted this to anyone, maybe not even to myself, but I'm in way over my head right now. The world laughed at my shenanigans for so long that I wanted to be taken seriously, and did anything I could to win. There's no way I could have won as a Democrat, and no one smokes enough pot to vote me in as an independent. Anyway, you're probably wondering why I asked you here?"

"To support you as a libertarian?" Thelma replied.

Frumpf spoke, "I have faced the fact I am not getting my daughter back. Those aren't even her ashes in that box; I couldn't dishonor her in that way. And I'm pretty sure even if Baba back there indulges me I still probably won't get my thing back. When I release my tax returns, exposing to the country who I have done business with, I'll be impeached on the spot."

"Wow, quite an admission. So how is it I can help you?" Thelma gingerly inquired.

Frumpf smiled for the first time since she entered the room, and said,

"Can you show my chef how to make your gefilte fish," he replied.

We were all sure Thelma was pulling our leg, and even after she insisted she was on the level it was hard to believe. Frumpf told her that the story of two of his agents raiding her fridge moved up the ranks. Snopes asked Thelma how she responded.

"I gave him an ultimatum," she replied with a straight face.

We all laughed at what we assumed was Thelma making light of our current situation. But she continued,

"I told him I would if he legalized marijuana."

When the news hit that Frumpf was behind the complete decriminalization of weed, the potheads went wild, but many saw the edict as a Hail Mary distraction tactic on the part of Frumpf to avoid having to release his taxes. We could not believe that Thelma accomplished in a five-minute meeting what marijuana advocates spent years and millions of dollars trying to achieve. If this was an attempt to take the nation's mind off of his taxes it was a much better gambit than the usual presidential tactic of declaring war somewhere. If only the answer to disguising corruption involved something beneficial to society, the world would be saved in a matter of months. What made it seem legit was Frumpf had already sent some aids on a hunt to source *all* of the ingredients to Thelma's famous dish. The good news was pot was semi-legal in Cambodia as Cambodians traditionally also used it as an ingredient in their Khmer cuisine that was influenced by the French, which no one brought up.

Thelma raved about the Air Force One kitchen that afternoon, going on about how impressive it was, and well-stocked with ingredients. She rated the pot Frumpf was able to acquire through a taxi driver as mediocre, but more than adequate for her recipe. She then told us Frumpf wanted us all to join him tonight for a grand gefilte fish dinner with King Norodom Sihamoni. Unlike the Cambodian Prime Minister Hun Sen, who had a history of corruption and was apparently seduced by greed, Cambodia's King was more seduced by the arts. Filmmaker, ballet teacher, and music scholar, Norodom was known through Europe as a respected cultural ambassador. None of that stuff mattered to Frumpf more than the fact he was about to entertain a real king. Had Frumpf had his druthers, he would have much preferred becoming a king than a president. No secret to anyone because Frumpf acted like a monarch.

In America wherever they serve ethnic food the environment is often decorated to reflect the origin of the cuisine. Mexican restaurants have colorful blankets and sombreros hanging on the wall, Chinese has calligraphy dragons and colorful lanterns, Italian has checkered tablecloths and wicker wine bottles, but how do you decorate for American food Frumpf wondered and sent his aid to ask us for advice.

Thelma immediately chimed in that gefilte fish is Jewish cuisine, adding that Frumpf's grand example of circumcision would be more than enough to represent that theme.

The King was respectful. Aware that Frumpf was sans first lady, and had just lost his daughter, he came solo as to not rub his royal family happiness in the president's face. Unfortunately, unbeknownst to all of us, Frumpf's plan for the King was quite the opposite. The King certainly knew how to hold court, captivating our attention with tales of his regal travels, and studies in Prague and North Korea. Frumpf had little to say and appeared marginalized by our fascination with our royal guest. When dinner was served, Frumpf's plate had a tiny serving of gefilte fish, but the King's portion was enormous. When his highness pointed it out, Frumpf claimed he was on a diet, but encouraged the King to "chow down."

Diet?! The closest Frumpf came to something that even resembled a diet was having two pieces of cake instead of three. It became unbelievably apparent to me that Frumpf was about to dope the King.

Who does this? What kind of man would spike a courteous Cambodian Royal with pot-laced whitefish just to offset his stature? I could only surmise his missing penis created an enormous lack of self-esteem and his devious mind was constantly scheming ways to make up for it. Thelma was suspicious, being guilty in the past of spiking a blackmailing Snopes herself. She took immediate action and sneezed in the direction of the King's plate. Apologizing profusely, Thelma took his plate into the kitchen and immediately returned with a fresh platter. What Frumpf did not realize was Thelma had made some non-spiked portions, which is what she now served to the King.

As the evening progressed, Frumpf was beginning to get very stoned. He planned on taking only a few small bites, but his routine voracious appetite got the best of him. Frumpf sat around like a fat zombie while the King continued to captivate us with candid tales of the underpinnings of Cambodian politics. When Frumpf proudly shared what he did to humiliate the Queen of England, Norodom seemed embarrassed and let on that *Elizabeth* has been overly accommodating to him when he and his family visited the UK. He even shared a story about how they got to ride in the lavish, gold-plated Diamond Jubilee State Coach, an unintended Frumpf touché. While Frumpf nodded out in his seat, the King told us that he had been following our pilgrimage. He claimed that in addition to all the phallic carvings and deities at the river, there was a large stone alligator that is considered a guardian of the spirit. It was his opinion that for the holy water to accomplish our goal for a man such as Frumpf, we needed to be sure that the carving of the aquatic lizard was completely submerged.

When I asked why, he said,

"Evil is often seen as a supernatural force. The site of Frumpf may cause the alligator to take a symbolic bite out of the flow you will need to accomplish your miracle."

Imagining a rock croc taking a bite out of anything would normally seem a bit on what Thelma would call the "hoobeedo" side, but after what I've experienced I was appreciative to have that information, and I thanked him for the insight.

The King said he would love to host us at his residence sometime and thanked us for a lovely evening. He confided that he had heard Frumpf was not the smartest or most aware grain of rice in the field, but hoped that the power of collective humanity find a way to inspire his compassion to enhance global prosperity. As we bid him goodnight, we all had the same thought, that we wished Frumpf was that kind of King.

*89

Norman was perplexed as to why the exclusive private banking department of his financial institution would invite him for a special meeting. His curiosity was quelled when the doting bank president presented him with the many special privileges his deposit of one million dollars afforded him. When Norman wrote to Thelma about being fired he had no idea this is what she meant when she claimed she would handle it.

Pauline's only response when Norman shared the news was,

"Maybe now we can support the arts instead of just appreciating it."

90

Absolutely everything regarding Frumpf's dick dilemma was covered by the press, which is why all of the news stations proudly broadcasted what that Dalai Lama called:

FRUMPF'S CURE

The video showed the Dalai Lama standing alone on a hilltop overlooking the canopy of the surrounding cedar forest. He peered directly into the camera and began his address,

"The world is out of balance when we are multiplying rapidly but remain divided. We do not need religion to convince us what our heart already knows without words, as no child waits for a book to teach them how to walk. Our greatest enemy has been the same throughout history, ourselves. And to conquer oneself is the greatest victory. To justify ongoing wars we have designated people as insurgents, terrorists, and radicals, yet compassion has somehow become the radicalism of our time. Without compassion, all that remains is ignorance, and with ignorance as our master there is no possibility of real peace. If you haven't already learned, the past is gone, we cannot turn back the clock, and the best we can do is use the present well. In the spirit of world harmony, and bridging the divide that is crippling humanity, I am formally inviting President Richard Frumpf and my good friend Baba Dickster to join me here in Dharamsala for a healing session that will once and for all prove to the world that our obstacles can be used as a source of strength, and the only true disaster is when we lose hope."

As we all stared at the screen, Thelma broke the silence,

"Holy shit, the Dalai Lama called you his good friend!"

Frumpf looked at me and just said, "Well?"

I hoped the Dalai Lama solution was better than his last attempt when he just recited one line in the temple, but I was certainly relieved now that the whole penis rejuvenation fiasco wouldn't be perceived as solely my responsibility. Snopes insisted the Dalai Lama had something up the sleeve of his robe because by claiming he had a solution to something risked not just his status, but also the reputation of Tibetan Buddhism itself. With that in mind I looked Frumpf in the eye and said,

"If the Dalai Lama wants to help you, I will do all he asks to assist him."

Frumpf was encouraged and said he was going to notify the staff to get this aluminum hotel back in the air, and on its way to India.

Air Force One was greeted with complete goodwill and major fanfare. Frumpf would find no need to spin it because the crowds were truthfully large and outwardly loving. Gone were the protest signs comparing him to Hitler. Instead of demonstrators voicing their disapproval, the air was lacquered with the passionate chants of devoted monks. It is customary for Buddhist renunciants to be calm, courteous, and respectful to all, so Frumpf was way ahead of the game. The prayer flags were streaming, and as we disembarked together, we were showered with flowers presented by monks wearing their saffron robes and the outlandish yellow Mohawk-looking hats of the Gelugpa. I don't know what any of this will have to do with getting his dick back, but it was obvious if a miracle were possible this was the place because right before our eyes we saw Frumpf do something for the very first time, he laughed.

Back in the states news footage of our jubilant tarmac reception by the most peace-oriented entity in the world was what the country needed after weeks of feeling like we were on the verge of the apocalypse. A week ago, Google searches for world war 3 and Frumpf's war hit an all-time high, now the most popular search was a term made popular by news anchor Henderson Cooper when he called our host's speech the "Dalai Lama Penis Promise."

As usual, the corporate world aimed to capitalize on the commotion and revamped their websites with a Tibetan flair. Buddhas were everywhere. Some businesses went too far like the famous motel chain whose slogan was now, *Come NamaSTAY with us!*

Not only was Frumpf in good spirits, but even his physical prowess gained a bounce from the steroids his self-esteem received through the monk's unconditional reception. We marched uphill along a pristine mountain trail for a mile, and the president didn't stall or complain once. When the trail forked, the procession veered off to the left upon a large empty field where a contingent of monks was hard at work creating a large colorful mandala. According to Buddhist scriptures, mandalas transmit positive vibrations to those that view them. During the mandala's construction, the monks chant and meditate to invoke divine energies from the deities residing in the design. The monks then ask the deities for healing blessings. It was explained to us by one of the monks that in this case all of the healing power would be extended towards Frumpf, which explains why the unfinished outline in the center of the mandala resembled a penis.

I had to hand it to the Dalai Lama, we have only been here for an hour, and he already had Frumpf smiling, laughing, hiking, and reveling in the reality that a powerful spiritual sect was avidly working to help him regain his manhood. After a small ceremony at the mandala site in which a group of monks circled Frumpf on their knees chanting towards his crotch, we were escorted to a nearby group of beautifully adorned tables and invited to share in a tantalizing vegetarian feast. Frumpf claimed it was the tastiest food he had ever eaten. When the lunch was over, we were escorted back to the plane and told we should relax and be calm, with no further instructions.

Yuva Yatree may be the first Buddhist in history to have turned down a direct request from the Dalai Lama. It wasn't that what the holy man was asking of him was impossible or out of his realm of ability, it just posed a dilemma that was unique to Yuva himself. Yuva had been seen by the monks as a gifted healer, a reputation he got from supposedly ending a flu epidemic that ran rampant through Dharamsala using only music as his medicine.

The sun had not quite set, but as it descended towards the night, the light reflected off of the top of the cedars creating and ambiance that had Yuva and the Dalai Lama sitting silently on the veranda absorbing the energy of nature. The Dalai Lama broke the silence,

"Healing does not require revealing. You will appear as the mere breath of a sage, and vanish like a whisper in the wind."

"I know your ways master, and this is more about me than him. You believe I am in line with a cosmic sequence, do you not? You have never been one to accept light as coincidence," Yuva replied.

The Dalai Lama nodded and pondered the young man's words. Yuva continued,

"I would give my life to preserve yours, but I fear the ramifications of reuniting with my past."

The past Yuva referred to was ten years ago when at the age of thirteen, he, little Brucie Timinsky decided that instead of adhering to the Jewish Bar Mitzvah tradition of suddenly becoming a man, he became a monk. Under the veil of being just another monk in a crowd of many, he was able to view his mother today for the first time in a decade. He was quite surprised to see Thelma looking younger and more beautiful than he remembered.

"Yuva, you cannot reunite with something that no longer exists. Who we are now is all that matters, and to experience the love that connects us," the Dalai Lama claimed as he playfully came face to face with Yuva, and momentarily touched foreheads.

Yuva agreed to participate in the ceremony the Dalai Lama had planned for Frumpf that in reality was more of a reunion between Yuva, Thelma, and Norman who was now resting in a guestroom with Pauline after a long flight.

Frumpf kept stopping by our cabin to see if we heard anything as if the Dalai Lama would contact Baba Dickster first. His good mood had already dwindled because he felt a bit slighted that the Dalai Lama hadn't greeted us himself. I reminded Frumpf of his own rudeness when the revered monk met with us in Washington. Frumpf was defensive and claimed he was preoccupied with his missing dick, to which I replied it is possible the Dalai Lama has the same excuse right now, reminding Frumpf his missing genitalia is the current focus of all of Dharamsala, if not the whole damn world. This helped to regain some of his composure. I thought no man's penis should ever get this much attention. I suggested we all watch the evening news to see how they covered this.

DAY 1 OF THE DALAI LAMA DICK CURE

Frumpf enjoyed watching even MSNBC revel at the warm reception he received. He noticed the extra bounce in his step as they showed us hiking the trail to the mandala. I think they went a little far in using computer graphics to turn the outline of the penis in the center of the mandala into a question mark, but that was the mystery on everyone's mind; will the Dalai Lama illustrate the true power of hope, and help Frumpf regain his dick?

To every dark cloud there is a silver lining, and in today's reactive world the opposite holds true. The attention Tibetan Buddhism was receiving as a spiritual healing power did not make the church leaders happy. The Vatican and associated dioceses were already miffed at Frumpf for his insensitive Grotto antics that promoted the fact their healing springs were incapable of his penile resurrection. Now, if this dick deed proved to be successful, the president would be telling the world that Buddhism was the most powerful religion in the universe. The Vatican wasn't having it and decided the only way to immediately take the spotlight off of the Dalai Lama was to air a message from the Pope himself.

Media outlets were having a field day as the controversies relating to Frumpf's missing dick gave them better ratings than the many scandals involved when he had one. When they promoted that Pope Francis was going to address the citizens of the United States regarding Frumpf's penis problem, everyone tuned in.

After waving to all, the Pope began his oration,

"This morning I was called by the Dalai Lama, a man I respect for his promotion of human compassion and commitment to global unity. He was not really calling on me, but through me, he was calling on God. He understands although meditation and chanting have their place in calming the world, and bringing inner peace, it does not possess the same healing power that is inherent through the hands of Jesus Christ our Lord and Savior. I have agreed to ask you all to pray with me that our God, through his love and divinity comes to the aid of mortal kindness by using his grace and power to heal president Frumpf so he may lead us all to achieve a stronger Christian nation. Thank You, and God Bless you all."

The Dalai Lama found it curious that he was one of the last people to learn he had called the Pope and was amused by what he saw as the Church's desperate attempt to remain prominent, so now if he healed Frumpf the Pope would get at least equal credit. More upset by the Pontiff's address were the other religious factions that took offense the United States was described as a Christian nation. It's not that it isn't common knowledge most Republicans act like their chambers are a manger, but the other religious leaders hate hearing it. I was skeptical that the Dalai Lama had called on the Pope to harness God's power. Even harder to believe was that religious leaders were now competing for credit for regenerating Frumpf's dick, something I alone had made disappear. If there really is a God I doubted he would spend one second dealing with Frumpf's crotch.

Just when we thought things couldn't get any weirder, the president of China called the president, and Frumpf let us listen in on his speakerphone.

"Hello President Jinmingpingling, you know what I'm trying to say, this is Richard Frumpf. How are you, sir?" Frumpf winked at us as if we were in on a prank call.

"I am not so happy. You know we exile Tibetan monks from Mainland China, and we see your affiliation as bad diplomacy," harped the Chinese President.

"I understand my friend, and excuse me for saying so, but we are talking about my penis here." Frumpf swallowed a chuckle due to the bizarre nature of this official conversation. Then continued, "What would you have me do in this situation?"

"Why are your penises so important in America? Can't you wait four years until it is not on the international radar? We have technology to make you a perfect temporary copy," the Chinese president stated.

We could not believe what we were hearing. Frumpf shrugged at us, unsure of how to respond. Thelma wrote something down and showed it to him.

"Four years is a long time without a cock my friend, and 2017 is your calendar year of the Rooster," said Frumpf.

Click.

We weren't sure if the Chinese president hung up mad, or somehow the reality that it was, in fact, the astrological year of the cock, threw him for a loop, but Frumpf gave Thelma a thumbs up for her creative intervention.

Rhoda, who has remained relatively quiet throughout our international adventure, was happy snapping photos with the hi-resolution camera we purchased for the trip to keep a journal of the experience, which she claimed could become another bestseller when this bizarre expedition was done. While she gave us a little preview of some of her favorite shots, Frumpf's aid informed us we had a visitor on board. We were perplexed and joked that the way things were going it might be Jesus himself. Although not the case, it was someone Thelma used to see religiously, Norman and Pauline. When the momentary shock wore off, we all hugged and sat down. Thelma immediately began the questioning,

"What are you guys doing here Norman?"

Norman looked into the eyes of the woman who is still his wife, and with a serious tone said,

"I need you to sign divorce papers."

Before Thelma could respond Norman broke out in laughter claiming although that was true, he didn't have them with him, and it was not really why they were there. He said the Dalai Lama himself called him insisting he be here for what he described as a spectacular surprise, then without missing a beat, Norman thanked her for the generous augmentation of his bank account. Thelma said she should thank me, but I told him I had heard he lost his job over all this, and he certainly deserved some of the book loot for his invaluable participation getting us to this point. I also thought that landing Thelma was at least worth that much, but kept that to myself. Norman then realized that only Thelma had met Pauline, and officially introduced us all.

"So, anyone have an idea of the big surprise," Norman asked.

Everyone shook their heads no, but with the advent of Norman's arrival, I had a strong suspicion. When I met with the Dalai Lama in D.C., I asked him for a small favor. I described the details in which Brucie Timinsky vanished to Tibet, and said if he ever hears about anyone that fits the description I would appreciate the tip. It appeared that not only had he located him, but he also planned to reunite him with his parents. I probably should have kept Thelma in the loop about this, but I didn't want to get her hopes up needlessly, and now I certainly didn't want to meddle in the Dalai Lama's deeds, which was apparently now the job of the Pope.

A procession of robed disciples arrived to escort us on another jubilant parade to the mandala site. Throngs of chanting monks surrounded the mandala in a semi-circle. The mandala was now complete and featured the most incredible depiction of male genitalia anyone had ever seen. The monks guided Frumpf to the base of the mandala and had him sit facing it. They instructed him to stare at its core without taking his eyes off it, and to imagine the energy of the phallic image penetrating his being. Frumpf was so taken by the possibility of regaining his dick he would have blown the monk if that were what it would take.

While Frumpf stared at the mandala, Thelma and Norman were shepherded away to a clearing on the other side of the trail where they were greeted by the Dalai Lama.

"Welcome, Norman and Thelma. A while ago Baba Dickster asked a favor of me. He first told me a story about your lost boy, Brucie."

His comments were interrupted by the sound of Thelma gasping at the fact the Dalai Lama uttered her son's name. He smiled and continued,

"It is my belief the past is like a rose, once the petals drop it is no longer a flower, but it is still something. Your son is no longer little Brucie Timinsky, but instead of dropping his petals I believe you will agree he has now become a flower."

From behind a cedar stepped the tall, handsome Yuva Yatree. Norman was in shock, but Thelma wasted no time and rushed right into his welcoming arms. Yuva looked over to where the Dalai Lama had stood, but he was gone. Thelma opened one side of the hug and motioned for Norman to join in the embrace. A faint mystical glow appeared to surround them as they reveled in their perfect reunion.

Frumpf still sat staring at the penile nucleus in hope. The Dalai Lama suddenly appeared at the top of the mandala. The president looked up at him.

"What have you learned," asked the Lama.

Frumpf said for some reason he kept thinking about the waterfall at Penis River.

"Then that is where your hope resides. You must return, and complete your meditation there," the Dalai Lama insisted.

Yuva Yatree appeared with his string instrument and sang a song to Frumpf in Hindi. As the song progressed, the monks began to destroy the mandala by fanning the colored sand away with large fronds. When the mandala was gone, Yuva walked up to Thelma and Norman, who introduced him to the rest of the group.

Yuva escorted Thelma and Norman to his cabin in a small field on the side of the cedar mountain. He sat on a rock and played them a sweet song he wrote about their impending reunion that gave them joy. He told them that his dream was to turn his little bit of heaven into a center where people learned to heal through music, which is an ability he had nurtured for the last ten years. He claimed he was aware they were no longer a couple but said they would always be his parents, a partnership that was impossible for them to erase. When Thelma asked the significance of the name Yuva Yatree, he said,

"That is simple mother, it is the name that was given to me when I first arrived, it means Young Traveler."

The concept of spirituality is laced with ideas like honesty, compassion, and love. I call them ideas because how we adhere to those principles in our lives depends on the individual's interpretation, very similar to a musical style we all know as jazz. I compare it to jazz because what the Dalai Lama was about to do could only be seen as a unique improvisation. When Frumpf was escorted to the Dalai Lama's residence, he was greeted by Deva, by far the most beautiful young woman he had ever laid his eyes on. Her satin skin seemed destined for touch, and her black hair swayed like the mane of a storybook mare. When he looked into her green crystal eyes, he imagined her as the ultimate treasure of a king. As they waited for the Dalai Lama's arrival, she made him aromatic tea that seized his senses. She slowly moved around the room in a dancelike motion that accentuated every sexy nuance of her flawless body. Deva informed Frumpf she thought it ironic that sex has destroyed many political futures when in her mind it is politics that destroys one's sexual future. She then coyly asked him what kind of future he desires. Frumpf was enough of a veteran cocksman to know when a woman was a sure thing and immediately became all too aware he needed to regenerate his genitalia more than ever. As he contemplated how to reply to her question without sounding as sleazy as his thoughts, the Dalai Lama appeared, and Deva departed. To Frumpf, the great spiritual master's presence didn't hold a candle to Deva's sudden absence.

When Frumpf insisted I speak with him alone in his suite, I was pretty sure he was going to demand we go back to Cambodia and complete the missing part of the pilgrimage without having to release his taxes first. He poured me some kind of berry nectar he claimed the Dalai Lama just gifted him and said,

"First off I would like to thank you for indulging me, and my narcissistic tendencies. As I sat staring at the center of the mandala many things passed through my mind. On this trip alone I have offended the Church, the Queen, the French President, a King, China...you get the idea. I am done with all of that. My daughter is gone, my wife wants a divorce, and over half my country wants me imprisoned. As the Dalai Lama might say, 'The Universe may be giving me a hint that my path isn't perfect.' You no longer have to insist on my tax returns because I have decided to step down as president as soon as the pilgrimage is over."

His demeanor seemed sincere, but there was no doubt in my mind he was a top tier conman. In this case, he wasn't lying about his intentions, only the reasons, one reason, Deva.

"How do I know you are not saying that just to get me to complete the pilgrimage without performing your side of the deal," I replied sternly.

"Baba, the Dalai Lama is asking me to trust the universe, all I am asking you to do is to trust me," he wisely stated.

Had we not been relegated to a cabin that mimicked first class on a commercial airline, Thelma would have ravished my body in gratitude. She told me I was the most thoughtful human being on the planet, and she would spend the rest of her life making me happy. She said the reunion with Yuva and Norman was not only a miracle, but she believed it completely cleared the emotional path for her and Norman to move on in the spirit of love. She shared that we were welcome to visit Yuva anytime, and hoped someday to help his dream come true. I told her she had the Dalai Lama to thank, but she insisted that in her eyes Baba Dickster was her spiritual master, a master she couldn't wait to supplicate herself in front of.

Snopes and Rhoda had an amazing experience wandering the grounds, photographing Dharamsala. Snopes said he needed a break from the drama to clear his head and think everything through. It was of his opinion we should complete the pilgrimage regardless of whether Frumpf planned on keeping his word. At this point, none of us were aware that all the president was thinking about every waking moment was getting his dick back so he could consummate his desire to possess temptress Deva.

We decided it would be inhospitable to not invite Norman and Pauline to tag along for the rest of the journey. We imagined even if they don't participate in the final ceremony, the two artists would take extreme delight in wandering the stone temples and colorful markets of Siem Reap. They graciously accepted our offer.

91

The road to the waterfall at Penis River had been repaired quickly to accommodate the sudden rush of tourism our pilgrimage inspired. Thelma, Rhoda, Snopes, two Secret Service, three members of the media, a guide, Frumpf, and I drove towards the final leg of our pilgrimage. It occurred to me I spent so much time wondering if Frumpf was going to renege on his part of the deal I ignored that Baba Dickster was possibly the greater charlatan. I was now worth thirty million dollars and counting, all from a book that was mostly nonsense. And here I was about to go through the motions of being a radical magician pretending I could pull a penis out my hat with the whole world watching.

The cameras, audience, river, and Frumpf were all ready. I was not. I told them I needed a moment alone to meditate and center my powers. I sat on what I thought was a large rock that turned out to be the back of the stone alligator the King said needed to be submerged. I closed my eyes, and let the hypnotic drone of Penis River have it's way with me the way Lana had taught me to at the river back in Woodstock. I could feel the river rise around me enough to submerge the symbolic lizard. A group yelp made me open my eyes to see I was now surrounded by hundreds of turquoise butterflies. After a minute they all winged over to the waterfall lagoon. As cosmic a time as any, I motioned for Frumpf, who now looked like a caricature the way his naked round belly drooped over the tight waistband of his swimsuit, to follow me on a short walk over the stone carved phallic riverbed.

When we reached the lagoon, I instructed him to completely disrobe, for no other reason than making that fat fuck expose his flabbiness to the world. Anxious to be reunited with what he now thought of as his *Deva Dick*, he took off his suit with his saggy ass towards the cameras. The water temperature felt colder than I remembered, and I joked to myself that instead of inflating Frumpf's dick I was going to shrink mine. As we sat in the pool under the gentle falls facing the wall of the grotto, Frumpf broke the ceremonial trance claiming he had felt something. With my finger to my lips, I silently implored him to remain quiet and pointed his attention towards the same grotto wall where I had seen his image the last time I was here. After five awkward minutes, that to the dickless president was an hour, the force of the falls began to increase establishing a heavier mist around us. An image began to appear on the wall. I looked over at Frumpf, and it was evident that he was also witnessing something. When the image became more defined, it became obvious that it was the formation of the penis design from the core of the Dharamsala mandala. Just as it became crystal clear, the force of the falls increased to the point of submerging us in the pool.

The audience was momentarily alarmed as we vanished, but a minute later the falls went back to its original feeble flow, and we resurfaced. As everyone watched in suspense, Frumpf reached down to touch his submerged crotch and then leaped forward to give me an exuberant hug. As his naked groin brushed against mine, I was relieved to know our pilgrimage was successful, but would have chosen a different method of confirmation. Frumpf was so excited that he rushed over to the riverbank, climbed up on a large stone, and proudly presented his penis in an inauguration whose number of attendees this time mattered not.

When the news media broadcasted Frumpf's penile reunion in its entirety, the whole world went nuts. There wasn't a communication device on the planet that didn't portray his naked rock pose on the screen. Never before had a crotch gone through so much fanfare and scrutiny.

*92

Done with Air Force One, the six of us decided to check into a luxury hotel in Siem Reap recommended by the King. Thelma had immediate lewd intentions that under ordinary circumstances I would have welcomed with open legs, but not only was my energy depleted from the ceremony, my dick still recovering from its unsettling brush with Frump's, but I was also preoccupied with the reality that it was time to kill Baba Dickster. As famous as Frumpf's penis may have become, I was the sorcerer who reclaimed it. People would soon seek me out non-stop. What I told Thelma next was heartbreaking. Had we thought it all out in advance, Thelma and I would have made sure we were never seen together. Now when I remove my Baba Dickster disguise to become plain old Sheldon Gross, my anonymity will be outed by my proximity to her. Through her tears, she insisted we could go somewhere remote until the heat and attention died down. I explained that in this *Kardashianized* society, the paparazzi would find us, and then I will have to hide forever. As we lay in the beautiful bed, Thelma held me like she would never let go. When she woke up, Baba Dickster aka Sheldon Gross, magic penis manipulator, and millionaire author was gone.

*93

When Frumpf announced he was stepping down to spend time in India, people all over the world were ecstatic, except of course the people of India. Having no family to return to, Frumpf had Air Force One drop him off near Dharamsala. Being that his dick was basically brand new, Frumpf saw himself as a virgin committed to remaining so until he reconnected with Deva, a reunion that would never come to pass. The former president pleaded with the Dalai Lama to help him find her, but getting Frumpf to step down to chase an impossible dream may have been the Dalai Lama's plan all along, we will never know for sure. And honestly, I had already reunited Frumpf with his greatest love.

A month later, former president Frumpf, a man whose penis captured the attention of a sexually obsessed world, unlikely marijuana liberator, and royal prankster, died when on a caravan in search of Deva, broke his neck falling off of an elephant; a fitting end to a man that climbed onto the back of Republicanism just to further an avaricious agenda.

*94

I arranged for Snopes to be in charge of what I considered "our millions," with instructions to be sure Thelma, Ella, Angela, Norman, Rhoda, and he, had access to whatever funds they needed to use as they saw fit. He set up an offshore account with ten million for me, which I had already begun to use to help Syrian refugees in need. Snopes finally cracked the Cuka code, and with the help of Ella, Angela, and his new bride Rhoda, marketed non-GMO seeds for the nutritious new vegetable worldwide.

*95

Two years later, as the India sun set over a hillside musical healing center surrounded by towering cedars, Thelma and Yuva Yatree enjoyed their annual "Penis colada" to toast my efforts in bringing them back together. In the distance, they saw the Dalai Lama approaching with what appeared to be George Clooney. Thelma suddenly rose to her feet, and with a look only love can inspire, flew into my arms and mated with my soul forever.

The End

I hope you enjoyed TRUMPING FRUMPF. I would appreciate it if you would submit a review to Amazon, and share the link on Twitter, Facebook, etc. THANK YOU!!!!

This is a work of fiction. Names, characters, businesses, places, events, and incidents are either the products of the author's imagination or used in a fictitious manner. Any resemblance to actual persons, living or dead, or actual events is purely coincidental.

ABOUT THE AUTHOR

Buddy Winston *is a writer, comedian, musician, and artist. He is a former staff writer for the Tonight Show with Jay Leno and has performed as a stand-up comic all over the world. His last book, a novelized autobiography* **"An Out Of Buddy Experience"** *is available on Amazon. Buddy resides in the Ecuador Andes next to the Equator with his two dogs.*

BuddyWinston@gmail.com

http://www.WordsOfWinston.com

www.ingramcontent.com/pod-product-compliance
Lightning Source LLC
Chambersburg PA
CBHW070831310526
45788CB00017B/372